Contents

Turning Trials Into Triumphs-- The Way of the Phoenix
A Guide to Personal Empowerment Through Coping Strategies and Life Skills

www.MyNameIsPhoenix.com

www.FromVictimIntoVictor.org

Cover Design: Lana "Jazmyn" Stewart, Artwork by: Lana "Jazmyn" Stewart

For your *FREE GIFT* visit: **www.MyNameIsPhoenix.com**

If you were helped by a Chapter in this book, or the whole thing, I invite you to write a positive review on Amazon.com **now.** This helps other people to find me, and to feel confident about purchasing my book.

This book may help your business or group to become more productive, healthy individuals. If you want to purchase books in bulk, or to contact me, email me here: MyNameIsPhoenix2@gmail.com

What the Phoenix Means to Me...

As a young child, I was taken to the Phoenix Arizona Airport where I saw a huge mural with the Phoenix on it. I was told the legend of the mythical bird. This magnificent, unique bird willingly turns itself completely into a huge ball of fire to transform itself into an even more beautiful and majestic creature. Even as a five year old, I clearly understood the symbolism of this myth.

As I matured, I had many opportunities for tremendous growth through extraordinary adversity; and the myth of the Phoenix continued to resonate within me.

The Phoenix is richly symbolic in many spiritual traditions. The idea of willingly being consumed by fire (adversity) in order to free oneself and soar gracefully and freely like a bird is incredibly inspiring to me.

This bird is not a victim or merely a survivor—it is the embodiment of triumph over trials. To me, it represents the characteristics of wisdom in adversity, beauty, strength, and an indomitable will.

I feel empowered by owning this name. I strive to exemplify the strength, wisdom, and resilience that embody "The Way of the Phoenix."

The legend of the Phoenix is found in many cultures. What inspires me about the Phoenix is the way it voluntarily burns itself in order to create a new and better creature. It is a symbol of renewal, resilience and re-creation. The fire is a symbol of adversity to me.

- A Phoenix is always changing, growing, and becoming better. I invite you to Turn Your Trials Into Triumphs and Live the *Way of the Phoenix*.

Testimonials

"Turning Trials into Triumphs is a wonderful read for all who have dealt with adversity in life and seek new tools for use in coping with that adversity".

—**Marnie Dominy**, Author: *Choosing Your Healthy Path: How to achieve wellness and weight loss by following a successfully proven plan*

"This is not your ordinary self-help book! Phoenix peels back the outer, public layer of our lives to look at the underlying emotional turmoil and painful experiences that block many of us from enjoying our lives. Since we all experience problems, she believes it's how we choose to respond to them that determines whether or not we will experience true happiness.

"After reassuring us that not every trial or adversity is self-inflicted, Phoenix courageously shares some of the traumatic experiences she has overcome. Then she gives us healing steps to follow and guidance to overcoming our own. She believes if we listen to our intuition and connect with the divine, we can overcome even crippling adversity and find and live our true life purpose.

"In addition to traditional therapy, she has also used and thinks many can benefit from music therapy, aromatherapy, lucid dreaming, and bodywork. Whether you are getting out of caustic relationships or transcending how you were parented, she believes we all have more resilience than we think we have.

By reading this book, you will find your own triumphant strength and will be a witness to Phoenix's belief in the timeless truth that we are not tried above what we are able to bear. This book is a powerful series of stories and tested advice."

—**Flora Morris Brown Ph.D.**, Author: *Color Your Life Happy: Create the Success, Abundance and Inner Joy You Deserve*

"Author writes straight from the heart. This compelling read is full of heart-warming stories of how to stand up and be counted—even if it is only by yourself! Full of action steps anyone can use to make his or her life better.

"Helpful for anyone who wants to develop the principle of emotional self-reliance. Thoughtful commentary on how to make bad things better.

"Do you feel like a puppet on a string, and someone else is pulling the strings? This book can help!"

—**Karen Evans, Ph.D.**, Counseling Psychology, Licensed Psychologist

"I have known Phoenix now for many years now. We have exchanged thoughts and ideas and memories; some more painful than any human should have to endure. I believe she has put into words one of the most comprehensive guidelines to healing I have ever read. This is a God inspired message to all of humanity. I feel that anyone can read this book and bring from its message the answers they have been seeking-- that peace and fulfillment that life today drains from us. Phoenix has provided both an emotional and physical guideline for growth and rebirth. I pray that everyone finds this message as uplifting as I did. Phoenix, I thank you with all that I am for what you have given back to mankind. Well done Ma'am! I have never been more proud of any student ever! You are the example to follow Ma'am." Again well done!"

—**Ken Tork**, Black Belt Karate Instructor

"Get ready to be inspired to take positive action and realize your full potential! This book has a wealth of inspiring ideas for every personality, and relevancy for every life. For those who are generally proactive with life, re-fuel and gain new ideas and introspection here! For those feeling the overwhelming hopelessness of your impossible situation; here are the instructions for taking control. You CAN re-shape your future; open your mind and prepare to see a whole new world of possibilities. Step up to the challenge of creating your new life!"

—**Rebecca Morgenroth**, Realtor

"Phoenix writes with authenticity and courage. Her story of triumph is one of inspiration and hope combined with real-life applications you can begin using today! It is full of great strategies for making immediate and lasting changes in your life."

—**Kelly Buchanan**, BS, Licensed Massage Practitioner

"I once read that mighty men and women will be mightily tested and that the greater the trial that is overcome, the greater the lesson that can be derived. This book is an ultimate culmination of that truth. We all go through our own unique crucibles and this book and the principles in it have helped me to better understand and persevere through my own trials. The book is infused with power because you can feel the author is an authority in this area. I also loved reading the chapter about the "Job Principle" and how Job in the Bible was rewarded exponentially for enduring what should have been the unbearable pain of losing literally everything. The application sections throughout the book were invaluable, especially in the section about "Finding the love of your life." The insights I gained from this book have impacted my life in ways I can't fully describe in a short review."

—**Mike Snow,** Amazon 5 Star Review for 1st Edition

Book Review

"*Turning Trials into Triumphs* by Phoenix is an unforgettable self-improvement memoir that reflects one woman's spiritual quest and journey toward healing. As a survivor of unspeakable abuse she passes along what has helped her not only survive and thrive but triumph over all of life's challenges.

This book chronicles not only Phoenix's own journey towards healing from multiple forms of abuse and emotional trauma—and becoming a bodyworker—but the recovery methods that have worked for others. In no way is this book merely a personal rant against a history of surviving "personal" violence. It is written as a universal story for anyone who has confronted spiritual abuse and freed themselves from its tenacious grip.

Phoenix gives her reader not only a profoundly moving story of personal courage, survival, and the transformative power of a loving spirituality, she gives them tools (in workbook form) to work through their own doubts, fears, obstacles, memories, failures and personal horrors. The book is full of Phoenix's wit, hope, and honest foibles as well as her fresh (alongside tried and true) ideas for change.

Bodywork features strongly throughout this work but most thoroughly near the book's end. Phoenix's own experience of bodywork helped her not only recall and release horrific memories of childhood abuse, it helped her uncover her calling—something she believes was God's particular wish for her. She writes, "My belief and faith in God and my understanding of [this book's] principles gave me the courage to persevere in my trials. I believe they will give you inspiration to tackle your challenges."

Turning Trials into Triumphs offers quite a bit of spiritual language: words of hope, forgiveness, compassion and understanding of why people (and especially children) suffer. And yet not one line of her faith-filled testimony is spoken as the final "Truth" (with a capital "T"). Rather, her Christian framework is very inclusive and sensitive to diverse religious, racial, sexual and ethnic groups.

As a scholar of religion, gender and violence myself, I found Phoenix's vision for transforming violence through various self-improvement methods and skillful therapies to be a supportive complement to cultural and social understanding of violence in modern culture. *Turning Trials into Triumphs* teaches us more about love, spirituality, trauma, truth telling, and hope than all the self-help books combined. It is one of the bravest, most honest books I've read in years. Most importantly, this book is written for her readers even as much as it is spiritual journey of the heart. I applaud Phoenix's candidness and perseverance in her steadfast pursuit of the power of healing. Phoenix's readers will be as helped as they will be blessed by her triumphs over her own trials."

—**Jennifer Manlowe, Ph.D.**, Psychology and World Religion, Author of: *Faith Born of Seduction: Sexual Trauma, Body Image and Religion* (NYU Press, 1995).

Dedication

- My sister… I thank God for every day we have shared upon this earth. You are my strength, my fortress, my truest friend and companion. Without you I never would have made it! I'm so blessed to have my best friend in my best sister.

- My son… You are my jewel—the most precious "gift" I have been given in this life. You have brought my life immeasurable joy just by being in it. You have helped me to learn, stretch, and grow. Your playful, happy nature brings me joy and helps me lighten up when life gets intense. You are a truly great guy. I am so proud to be your mother.

- My daughter… You truly live each day in the "Way of the Phoenix. I am so proud of the way you have courageously confronted the people that have hurt you so deeply. You are an amazing young woman. Always know that I love you. You are so beautiful. I am constantly amazed at your ability to let your light shine through any darkness and difficulty you encounter. You gave me the joy of creating life in partnership with God.

- My Daughter in Law… Without the beautiful contribution of your artistic vision in creating the cover, this book would not be nearly as appealing. Thanks for sharing your talents. How blessed I am to have you as another choice daughter in my family. You make a wonderful addition to our family.

- My Grandchildren… You give my life more joy and meaning than I have ever known.

This book is my legacy to each of you. I hope what I have learned in this life, and passed on to you in this book, will benefit you as much as it has me.

My deepest appreciation goes out to each of my dear friends. You know who you are! I give special thanks to all those who helped with editing and reviewing this book.

Preface: How to Use This Book Effectively

This book is compiled in a reference format with each chapter almost a stand-alone book. You can easily refer to any topic that interests you without the need to read all the other chapters. The book builds on life-skills with each successive chapter to represent all I have learned to date about how to cope with great adversity and overcome a terminal illness. Use it however it benefits you most. I have included a lengthy table of contents to help you easily reference any topic you need.

Even if abuse and severe trauma are not part of your history or "trials in life" we all experience similar *feelings* as a result of the trials each of us have. Our personal trials test everything in us They make us seek out healing, and reach for anything that will help us feel better, and improve our lives.

I believe the principles found in this book have *universal application* regardless of your history and I invite you to share the lessons I have learned from the trials that were sent to me that made me a Phoenix. You can learn the "Way of the Phoenix" too.

A note from the Author: This book includes my personal experiences and the experiences of others who have touched my life deeply. Some of these people have suffered from prolonged abuse, low self-esteem, difficulties with employment and relationships, and other forms of great adversity.

I have known many people who have been the victims of severe and extreme abuse and assault. As we've shared stories, I was frequently asked to write a book about how I overcame my own trials.

Through the advice of an attorney, I have created the composite person "Jenny" who is a representation of actual, true experiences that people have personally shared with me. Many of the people who comprise "Jenny" have used and applied the principles contained in this book to great advantage.

I can relate to the pain of the experiences of the people who represent "Jenny" as I am completely familiar with the experience of trauma and victimization. Any similarities between the author's life and that of the imaginary person called "Jenny" are completely coincidental. Additionally, other names have been changed as I shared other people stories completely intact.

This book encapsulates many of the lessons I have learned from my own experiences with severe health problems, surviving deeply traumatic abuse and the difficulty in effectively standing up for myself in the past.

The experiences included in this book are only a fraction of the trauma and adversity that I have experienced. *I have very intentionally omitted many details for reasons of privacy, safety, and because rehearsing them seems to activate more negative experiences.*

The point of this book is not to share every detail of the horrors I've experienced in my life; but to acknowledge those trials, learn from them, and move forward.

The real focus of this book and the most important message is: Whatever your problems are; you can stop re-living, rehearsing, and repeating them and move on to a place of peace and full integration with the best things in life.

My Whole Message Is, You Can Get Over Whatever Happened.

I believe this book can show you how to Turn Trials Into Triumphs. I invite your feedback. Send it to:

MyNameIsPhoenix2@gmail.com

If you are a trauma survivor, you will want to read my companion book:

"From Victim Into Victor The Ultimate Guide To Overcoming Trauma, Abuse and PTSD.

It has all the personal stories of overcoming abuse that are not included in this book.

It is my gift to the world of trauma survivors, so you can live the life you deserve!

Available on Amazon and from the Author at: www.FromVictimIntoVictor.org

Disclaimer:

The purpose of this book is to provide information and to entertain. This is not a "cure all" or the ultimate source on this topic, but suggestions based on the author's experiences. The author and publisher are not providing professional services. If medical, psychological, or legal services are needed, please seek a professional provider. No attempt has been made to ensure that this book contains all the information available on the subject. The author and publisher are not liable or responsible for any loss or damage caused, or alleged to have been caused, directly or indirectly by the information contained in this book to any person or entity.

Caution: This book contains stories and examples of abuse, violence, and trauma; including examples of sexual, physical, and psychological abuse. **These examples are especially suitable for anyone looking to overcome trauma, stress, abuse, and adversity.**

The book has an adult theme and is intended for adult audiences. Reader discretion is advised. The Author and Publisher assume no liability or risk if you decide to read this book. Read at your own risk.

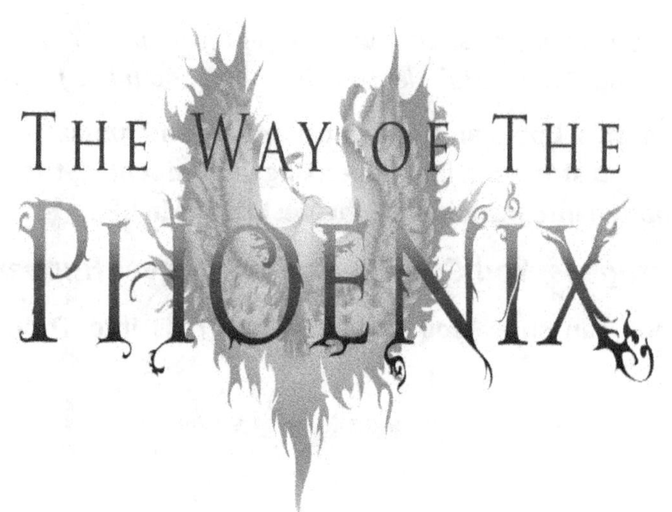
THE WAY OF THE
PHOENIX

Introduction

Here is a little background about me. I am a Personal Empowerment Guide (life coach) and licensed massaged therapist/bodyworker. I teach people how to overcome their limitations and difficult experiences to get what they want out of life!

I have been the sounding board for many individuals throughout my life as a friend, acquaintance, licensed massage practitioner and counselor. I happily share what has worked for me to solve my own problems. I feel the purpose of my life is to learn, share, and uplift others. If the only benefit to the adversity of my life is to share what I've learned with others and give love, empathy and compassion then it was all worth it.

I will share timeless truths I have learned through my own experiences. Many individuals have shared their pain and stories with me as I have interacted with them by helping them to release their trauma through bodywork and massage and coaching. I will also share some experiences of people with whom I have been a friend and confidante. I've assisted and encouraged them to transcend their difficulties through bodywork, empathy, and sharing the principles found in this book. All the names have been changed or omitted to protect the privacy of the individuals who have shared their experience with me.

I feel compelled to write this as a personal development guidebook to help and inspire the people whose experiences are contained in this book and for all of you who may be experiencing trials, and opposition of any kind. It is my deepest desire to give hope to others that they too will overcome any amount of difficulty and opposition with the right tools, mental preparation, and perseverance.

Through living the principles in this book I have triumphed over an incurable terminal illness and lived many years past my life expectancy. This happened because of my determination, faith, and the principles you will read in this book. You can find a path to personal triumph with the help of the suggestions found in this book.

My religion is Christianity. If this is not your religion, or if you have no religious affiliation, you will likely find similar teachings in your religion or in other philosophies. "Timeless Truths" are found in many religions and philosophies. However, they only work if they're completely true. Please adapt and apply these principles in whatever ways feel comfortable to you. I have predominantly used stories from the Bible to illustrate my lessons in the next few chapters. My belief and faith in God and my understanding of the following principles gave me the courage to persevere in my trials. I believe they will give you inspiration to tackle your challenges.

Enjoy your healing journey and breakthrough.

Emotional Wellness

How Our Trials Can Actually Help Us to Excel in Life

We each have a unique set of circumstances that we deal with that molds and forges our character. You decide whether adversity will break you or inspire you to claim the attitude, "There has to be more to life than this, and I'm going to find it!" You can choose the 'Way of the Phoenix.' Understanding the purpose of our trials creates emotional wellness and balance regardless of the circumstances in which we find ourselves.

Whatever our challenges, I believe that there are a limited amount of *feelings* that we feel in response to various situations we encounter. Feelings can vary in degree of intensity but they are still the same feelings experienced by someone else; in a similar, or possibly very different experience. **What we all share in common is feelings.** You will undoubtedly share the same feelings I have about something you have experienced in your life. This will help you identify with my struggles, or to the other's in this book. *The exciting news is that we can change our feelings by changing our thoughts and our behaviors will change as a result.* We don't have to remain stuck in the difficulties of the past or present. You can change your mind and change your life.

I want you to understand and then embody the resilience of the human spirit and the incredible ability residing within each of us that can propel us out of misery and difficulty into joy, success, achievement, and appreciation for all of life's experiences.

Whatever your particular circumstances, you can apply the principles found in this book to your life and achieve a greater level of understanding of their positive purpose. You can choose to triumph over your trials! As you read I want you to say to yourself **"If they can overcome their trials, I can too!"**

Here Are the Timeless Truths I've Learned

These principles have strengthened me in my struggles to overcome my own trials. I will expand on these concepts in the following chapters. I like to think of them as the gifts I've learned from my trials.

- **We are all born with an inner compass to guide us along our path.** Some call it inspiration, or intuition, some call it your conscience, or Universal Intelligence. You can learn to develop and use this guide in all you do to improve your life in unimaginably wonderful ways.

- **Each of us has life experiences that give us <u>exactly</u> the right opportunities for our highest growth.** The secret is to learn to turn the situation around and analyze it or reframe its meaning until you have gained the reward of the lesson the trial is trying to teach you.

- **Each of us has a specific purpose for our existence.** As we search for our life purpose and learn to use our skills and talents to elevate the lives of others, we will fulfill our grand design. We will receive extraordinary assistance if we are truly seeking to accomplish our life's purpose. We will be lead and guided along our path.

- **All experiences can work together for your good!** This has become my mantra; I believe it to my core. When you understand this principle, you will begin to see your perceptions about difficult experiences turn around, and suddenly your life becomes dramatically different. Each of us has undoubtedly known someone who allowed their adversity to make them bitter, unhappy people, while another with the same circumstances has used the adversity as a springboard for phenomenal achievement. The same boiling water softens a carrot and hard boils an egg. **The choice is yours. Will you choose to be better or bitter? It doesn't matter as much what happens to you, what matters most is how you respond to adversity. If you haven't found the good in the experience, it's not over yet!**

- **There seems to be a direct correlation between the magnitude of your problems and your potential for greatness!** If you seem to have monumental problems, it is likely that you are a person with *extraordinary strength and capacity to endure.* I believe the tests we are given in this life are for our good and in a strange way "fair." They may not seem like it at the time, but you will find the strength to endure if you will exercise responsibility, ask for guidance, and develop a sincere and unshakable desire to overcome. **The simple fact of life is: We are here to be tested and to learn.**

- **Not every trial or adversity is self-inflicted.** Some things happen because we need to experience them for our highest growth. The real "secret" is we are not in control of everything that happens to us. Not all of our trials are a result of negative thinking and poor habits of thought. Some adversity is designed by a wise and loving Creator who knows that truly great people refine themselves through trials and adversity. **Some experiences <u>are</u> self-inflicted because we continue in destructive habits and behaviors.** Some are just accidents, and others are the misuse of someone else's right to make choices. Sometimes adversity is caused by the enemy of light and truth trying to keep us from reaching our potential and giving up. Learn to change the behaviors and thoughts that hold you back or create self-inflicted misery. Learn to quit fighting the things you don't have control over that are designed for your growth.

- **When you master the art of changing your thoughts and perceptions, you can then master your emotions.** When you master your emotions, you can control your behavior. As you control your behavior, you can exercise true personal power. *Remember, the only thing over which you have ultimate control is your thoughts.* No situation can overcome you if you learn to control how you perceive and react to it.

- **We are here to experience adversity and its masterful purpose is to teach us to rise above it!** We are not here to wallow in self-perpetuated misery. Our trials are to help us to recognize the great talents and blessings that adversity can bring. Trials can help us develop latent talents and strengths we never knew existed.

- **You are here to be happy!** When you learn the immutable truths that bring true happiness and learn to cleanse your mind and body from the experiences that hold you back now, you will embody true peace, happiness and purpose.

- **If you're still alive, there is _ALWAYS_ a way for escape—whether emotionally or physically.** Don't get stuck where you are! There is always a way to deal with your situation. Don't despair, just keep looking for the answers and they will come! Escape may come in the form of "rewriting your history" or reframing the trauma of your life by finding a new way to look at it. **There is a way to find a benefit or lesson which set you free!**

- **Along with each trial comes a promise—you will not be tested or tried beyond what you can handle.** If you can internalize this truth, it will turn your thinking around. When you're hanging on by your fingernails you can look deep inside and find the inner courage to say, **"I CAN handle this or it wouldn't be happening." You can handle anything life throws at you! Too many people are ending their lives because they don't have suitable solutions. I want to stop this by providing real solutions and techniques to help you realize your potential!**

"Deserveability"

I think a crucial element in overcoming our trials is the basic principle that we deserve to be happy, healthy, safe, treated with respect, and have the financial resources to support our families and ourselves. We deserve all that life has to offer, provided we are doing our part to elevate human interactions and live by true principles. When you can say, "I deserve to be _______," you are on your way to achieving whatever you deserve.

Learn To Listen To Your Intuition

The foundation on which to build your life is following your true path to your authentic self. The lessons you learn in your life will be unique in the way they come to you but what you gain from it, "your lesson," will be found through listening to your inner voice of intuition.

We are all born with an inner compass to guide us along our path. I believe that as we direct our lives in a path of goodness seeking out and living true principles and providing meaningful service to others, we can keep this compass pointing to "true north". But, if we become casual in paying attention and following the direction of this inner compass, we will lose our direction and bearings. Eventually the directions will cease and the inner guide will no longer work.

If we give careful diligence to listening for this guidance, or inspiration, and then correlate our behavior with what we have been given, we will receive more and more guidance. A major purpose for our existence is to seek out and live true principles. Does it seem reasonable that we would be given the assistance needed to do that? I say emphatically—yes!

> **A major purpose for our existence is to seek out and live true principles.**

Some people call this guidance "intuition". I think of it as "inspiration" from a higher and wiser source—God. You may think of it however it feels right **for you** but know that we all have the ability to tap into a source of wisdom and guidance wiser than ourselves. I believe we are entitled to this guidance and that we will save ourselves a lot of anxiety running around chasing after things of less value to us personally if we will simply learn to listen.

If we learn to "read" people and trust our gut feelings, instincts and intuition, instead of our logical mind, they will reveal to us all we need to know about them for our good.

Following your intuition can keep you and your loved ones safe. You will be in the places you need to be, and gain information needed to assist you in your purpose and quest, as you follow your intuition.

> **Application: If you will learn to use intuition as a daily guide for your actions, and take time to meditate, and cultivate a deep reverence for inspiration and guidance, you can tailor your own action plan for success.**

Use your personal intuition to determine what is going to be of highest value in your quest to overcome your trials. Ultimately, we are all so unique in our experiences and temperaments that the things that will be life altering for me, may be different than the ones that shake your reality and cause you to move in positive new directions. You will find many suggestions in this book and through other sources about how to change your life and habits. You will have to decide which are most applicable to you. Learn to use intuition as a guide for every facet of your life.

What kind of things can we receive guidance about? We receive guidance about actions we should or should not take. We can be inspired about the specific actions needed to overcome a bad habit or improve a relationship with someone. We can receive warnings of imminent danger to us or to those for whom we are responsible. We can receive enlightenment about how to comfort and provide meaningful service to another. We can receive direction and insight into our own feelings and motivations, which is a crucial component of self-mastery. We can receive understanding about the thoughts and feelings of our spouse and children and those closest to us. We can be guided in a path we would not have considered on our own. *We can have pure knowledge pour into us that is not within our own experience or expertise.* Essentially we can be guided in everything we do **if** we are willing to listen and act upon what we receive as guidance.

Exercise: When you are wrestling with a problem "sleep on it". Your subconscious mind will try to work out the problem for you. When you first wake up in the morning and your mind is clear, ask your mind for the solution to your problem.

What problems do you currently need resolution for?

____

____

What insights come to you early in the morning?

____

____

What answers come in the restful state just before you doze off to sleep?

____

____

Exercise: Asking your mind out loud for the solution often brings a quicker answer. Take a few moments to really listen for the answer then write it down.

____

____

____

Here's an example of how that works:

I recently got a call from a friend in distress. She is a survivor of extensive and prolonged sexual abuse as a child. She said she has been dreaming about being raped as a child around **four** nights a week now for more than a month and she's freaking out because she's not sleeping well. Her question is, "Why am I having this recurring dream?" She mentioned how much work she has done to forgive the perpetrators and asked if I thought the dreams meant she had not really forgiven them. She hasn't had dreams like this in years. I thought about it and said I didn't think the dreams indicated that she had not forgiven them. I asked her, "What in your current situation reminds you of that situation?" She said, "I don't know." So I said, ask your brain the question out loud and I'll wait. So she asked her brain out loud while **I listened**. **She queried**, "What in my current situation reminds me of the things I'm dreaming about?" Then she paused for her brain to surrender the answer. In about 15 seconds she said, "Oh! I know! I feel totally out of control about the things currently going on in my life and the last time I felt like that I was being raped!" She didn't know the answer until she asked it out loud. Then as a follow up question I asked, "What situations or areas of your life could you say you have some control over? Then we focused on some actions and changes in her beliefs that would help her feel like she had some control over her life.

How do I know whether it's really inspiration or if it is just my own mind coming up with the solutions?

Ask yourself the following questions to determine the answer:

- What am I being guided to do?

- Does it make any sense?

- Would this be something I would normally think of on my own?

- How did the idea come into my mind, or what was I doing when I received the insight?

- Does the new thought require an action that leads me closer to my highest values or away from them?

- Does the inspiration cause me to reach for added emotional or spiritual strength?

- Is what I'm thinking about going to help or elevate my life or someone else's?

Here are some ideas about answering the previous questions based on my experience with inspiration and the counsel I have received from people who make it a high priority to seek for this inner knowing.

- If you can actually identify what action you need to take based on the thought you received, you are at a beginning point. This is good!

- Next, run the thought "past your gut". Some people think of the solar plexus, or the area just under the rib cage and diaphragm as the center of our emotions. It is here that I have a visceral response, like recoiling internally, when someone has malevolent intent toward me. It is here that I feel anxious when something is just not right. If what you're thinking makes you feel like you've done something really bad or acted against your highest values, or if it feels kind of sickening inside, or brings up intense reactions of "I really don't think I want to do this", it's time for further analysis. It may not be the right thing to do. Just as we can receive inspiration from our higher source, or God, our thoughts can be influenced by sources that would not lead us towards goodness, truth, or our highest values. **It often takes careful consideration to perceive truth from error. Frequently, the counterfeit is very close to the truth or is the "easier" path. The key is "tuning in" to your inner feelings.**

> **There are counterfeits to every true principle in the universe. Learn to discern the truth from the lies.**

Author's Experience: Several times, I have met someone for the first time in a context that would cause me to consider that person to have standards and values similar to my own (church). Yet, my initial reaction was that I felt my inner-self recoil from this person. I did not want to have anything to do with them. I immediately began searching my brain for possible reasons for this reaction, because I could find no **logical** basis for it. The individuals did not remind me of anyone else, or any other situation I had experienced and yet the feeling of repulsion was strong and undeniable. Within a few months, the reasons for these feelings became very apparent. As things began to unravel, one individual confided that he was being prosecuted for child sexual assault, *with his own child*, and another child. He pleaded for my help in acting as a character witness for him. I utterly refused. He was asking me for help after he had already confessed to the prosecution that he had done it. He was convicted and sentenced to **five** years in a maximum-security prison. Imagine what might have happened had I not been very careful not to expose my young children to him based on my initial reaction to him.

> **Sometimes the rational mind will overlook vital information that is available to the spirit or subconscious mind. This is especially true if you have been victimized before.**

Another individual began coming to my home and repeatedly asking me for food and substantial amounts of money. Again something didn't feel right and I felt protective of my family around him. I researched and found out that he was asking this of me despite being given generous donations from another source (church). I let the other source know what was going on. In about six months time he was investigated for stealing and forging checks. He also asked for assistance but I refused based on my feelings. In another instance, it was many years before I was able to understand why I felt such discomfort around a certain individual that I dated but chose not to have further involvement with. I never really felt safe around him. I later understood that he was involved in some very deviant activities. He often referred to himself as being "devious," but I thought it was just some kind of joke.

Application: Listen To Your Intuition and Don't Talk Yourself Out Of It!

Whether or not the inspiration/guidance makes any sense really depends on the context. Suppose I have been looking for solutions to increase my understanding of my child and enhance our relationship. I'm driving along absent mindedly, when suddenly I'm struck with several thoughts like:" They didn't understand my intentions in a given situation, or I had not adequately expressed my feelings to them, or possibly for the first time I began considering their point of view." It's probably inspiration. Act on it! I find that when a thought is inspired it's as if I know it throughout my whole being, as if at a cellular level. I believe this is how all the great discoveries have come about. A person has an idea come into his mind and after consideration they act on it. You may discover something vital by tapping into this source of guidance.

If I can say that I clearly would not think of this idea on my own, or it urges me to forgive more or stretch a little further with my compassion and change my perceptions, or possibly take some action I had not previously considered, I can feel that this is positive inspiration and act on it.

Sometimes the prompting requires immediate action!

Author's Experience: A profound example of this occurred for me when I was in my teens. I was taking a religious study class and it was around Thanksgiving time. I had an acquaintance in the class who I did not really consider a friend because she was so different from me. I couldn't quite figure out a way to bond with her. She had a lot of difficulties and was not very confident in herself or very popular with the other kids at school. In fact, she had been labeled as a "nobody or loser" by most of the other students. I had tried to include her in my activities and circle of friends because I felt like she really wanted to fit in and it is no fun to be left out. It cost me my friendship with a few of my friends. People can be so petty! Anyway, this particular day in class the teacher passed out three candy corn pieces to each student. We then sat in a circle and had to tell everyone what three things we were thankful for, and then we could eat the candy. As it neared my time to speak I had the urge to tell this girl that "I was thankful for her friendship and that I loved her." I really fought this thought because, while I loved her because she is a person of value, I was afraid if I said this, it would be misinterpreted by the other students or even her. I didn't really feel love for her like I did some of my other close friends, but as I wrestled with these thoughts my mind repeated, "Tell her you're thankful for her friendship and that you love her!" So I did.

> **Sometimes the prompting requires immediate action and a delay can have unforeseen and devastating consequences.**

She immediately let out a cry and began sobbing very hard. The teacher went over to comfort her and began talking with her as I sat wondering if I had done the wrong thing. Suddenly through tears she told the class and me,"I had a big fight with my dad yesterday and I hate my life. I decided that I was going to kill myself today!" I was stunned but thankful that I had acted on the words that had been placed in my mind!

The other students began to befriend her afterward and the teacher helped her to get some professional help to work through her problems. It's possible that she would have carried out her thoughts and taken her life if I had not acted on the inspiration and helped her to see she had value.

Lesson: So often we are <u>the only person</u> that can touch another individual at exactly the right time in their life. *Don't miss that opportunity!* This dramatic experience was a catalyst for me in learning to pay attention to my feelings and thoughts.

More than once in my life a friend has been at a crossroad contemplating taking their life and I have been prompted to call them or get together. What I learned is that they don't want to be talked out of it or told why it's wrong! They want to give a voice to their wounds, to be validated, to be accepted and to feel and see that you care! "Nobody cares how much you know until they know how much you care."—Teddy Roosevelt. Sometimes they just want to be comforted by a gentle touch to the hand, heart, or head to clear their thoughts and then as they move through their grief they find their own reasons to live. If they don't find a reason to carry on, you can't stop them from taking their life anyway. Do point them to appropriate professional help. The love of a friend is often the most potent healing. **Make it a life quest to save the life of another in whatever form you can.**

Exercise: Is there anyone that has crossed your mind lately when you weren't doing anything to remind you of them? If so who?

____

Take the time to make contact with that person and check in to see if they are okay. Call them and tell them they were on your mind and you wanted to check in with them. **Don't put it off. Do it now. Record your results.**

____

____

____

____

- If you are acting in a manner consistent with higher truths when you received the insight, it's worth acting on. If you were taking a "side road" and acting against what you believe to be right and the insight urges you to get back on track, do it! If you feel like you got a "wild hair" and think you ought to just toss out your higher values, think again.

> **Ultimately, there is accountability for the promptings we receive and ignore.**

- It is possible to dismantle this built-in guidance system when you act against it. Even hardened abusers who say they didn't know any better than to maim, rape, and kill have a conscience. When they first began the activities that lead them to the culmination of the heinous acts, they were warned and prompted against doing them. When they habitually ignore their conscience, they can move "past feeling" and lose their ability and desire to make correct choices. However, they are not guiltless in this, as they had already been warned. Ultimately, there is accountability for the promptings we receive and ignore. That may come in the form of suffering natural consequences for our actions, or by missed opportunities for growth, or a final judgment that I believe will take place after we leave this form of existence.

> **Some argue that because of being abused, some individuals are warped or somehow not able to control their actions or responses. I couldn't disagree more strongly!**

There are instances when a person guilty of a heinous crime has passed a polygraph indicating they are telling the truth. I believe in these cases, the person simply has no remorse for their actions. Their bodies don't register anxiety, rapid heartbeat, sweating, or changes in the inflections of their voice because they are *sociopaths*—they no longer care and are "past feeling."

> **Application: We can learn to control our thoughts, feelings, responses, and behaviors.** It is without question more difficult for those of us who have been abused, but we can and must rise above our circumstances.

There may be **rare** instances of severe mental illness that may be the exception to this rule. **One theory is that the severity of mental illness corresponds directly with the lack of personal responsibility for your own thoughts and actions.**

Warnings: Sometimes we receive intuition about events that take place in the future. Most often, these come as a warning.

Author's Experience: I have several examples of times when I received premonitions about events that had not taken place yet. When I left a university to get away from a professor who had sexually harassed me, I went to a different university in another state. I had been there only a few weeks when the most ominous feeling of foreboding danger enveloped me. **I had the distinct impression that someone was going to die and that it was inevitable.** I felt that nothing I could do would stop it. As I studied this out in my mind I couldn't think of any family members that seemed in imminent danger so I concluded that it must be me who was going to die. I didn't get the particulars of exactly how it would happen, just that it was going to happen immediately.

I thought about how I had lived my life and determined that I felt I could leave this life without regrets. I thought about what I needed to do in the final hours of my life and my thoughts turned to my family. I called my sister with whom I have an especially loving relationship and told her that I believed I was going to die. I shared how I was feeling and told her that I had called to tell her I loved her and say goodbye. She was very upset, of course, but I expressed the relative feeling of peace I had because I knew I would not have chosen to live my life differently than I have.

It turned out that it wasn't me scheduled to die—at that time. It was my sister's best friend, and former college roommate *who was murdered.* She lived in an adjacent city to where I lived and my sister was scheduled to come and visit her later that week. This friend had just become engaged to be married and was excited to share the details with my sister. Unfortunately, she had car trouble while doing some deliveries for her employer. An ex-convict took advantage of the situation and tried to rape her. She fought him fiercely, but he brutally stabbed her repeatedly and left her to die. She was found several hours later in her car—dead.

We were all horrified. I began to fear that her murderer might somehow link us together (since she was going to visit my sister) and that I was going to be the next to be killed. At her funeral the speaker told of how this young woman had told her roommates almost exactly the same things I had said to my sister, the night before. She would have seen my sister in a few days had she not been murdered. The murder was particularly devastating to my sister who later expressed to me that she felt I had said to her what her friend would have said to her if she could. She found enormous comfort in these words. Her murderer was later found and convicted. **It was about a year later that I experienced someone I knew very well who tried to murder me with a knife.** But I faced him down, escaped, and got a permanent restraining order against him. Perhaps because of this time of premonition, I had courage and could clearly think about how to escape.

Lesson: We can be prepared for unexpected crisis if we will listen to our inner voice.

Application: Learn to tune in to your intuition or gut feelings.

Spiritual Direction and Guidance

Author's Experience: I won't set myself up as a spiritual guide for anyone else. You will have to seek your own answers for your path. I can provide suggestions based on my experiences but you will have to be the ultimate judge of whether they are right for you.

Many of the timeless truths I have learned through prayer and meditation are universal and can be applied to many other situations.

Sometimes we receive direction and guidance, or are granted some vital information that is too private or sacred to share. Learn to keep some things to yourself.

I believe that others don't get to decide what spiritual experiences you are entitled to or what you deserve from life.

Application: We are all seeking for something beyond our own reasoning and physical senses to believe in and connect to. I believe a desire for spirituality is intrinsic in each of us.

This desire compels us to seek ways to connect to the divine, the unexplainable, and fill the void within us. This is a critically important need to fill. When you are seeking for truth, you will find it. Your path will be guided and you will be lead to the people, places and concepts that will fill this need. **Truth is truth whether we accept it or not.**

I experienced this phenomenon when I went for counseling with several therapists. They didn't want to interfere with "my process" and wanted me to come to my own conclusions about what I should do. I had no direction and I felt re-traumatized every time I talked about the time I was nearly murdered and other horrible experiences of my life. I felt the same physical reactions in my body as I did when they were happening to me the first time. If I knew how to fix it myself, I would have! I quit going to them because I was not getting better and I had to believe there was a way to get the trauma out of my body. I hope this is not the experience you have had. There are many fine therapists who can make a huge, positive difference. If you don't connect with a therapist in a beneficial way, find another one or try some other options like massage/bodywork. Because of my intense desire to find a way to get relief, **I found it** through a special kind of bodywork which helps release unresolved trauma in the mind and body. I will explain this in more detail in the chapter on bodywork. I now give this style of bodywork treatment to others.

Best and Worst Case Scenarios

As a young woman, I was introduced to the concept of problem solving by looking at the worst-case outcome and then working out a game plan to overcome it. If you know how you'll handle the worst, you can easily handle anything that's less challenging in dealing with that issue. In my youth, I tried applying this method but because of being stuck in old patterns of thought it was hard to figure out how to solve the "**new**" problems I was dealing with. It was not until I was older, with the advantage of being on my own, that "looking for the worst while planning for the best" really came into play. It worked successfully for me when I could figure out how to deal with the worst-case scenario. I was free to solve the problem and be joyous if the worst thing didn't happen.

Some people argue that most things we worry about never actually happen, so quit worrying about the hypothetical. Don't waste time worrying about something you anticipate in the future until you are actually faced with it and then you will have added resources you didn't know about in the beginning that will help to deal with it. The key here is to trust that you have what it takes to overcome anything you are faced with.

Most things I have anticipated and worried about have actually happened and not because I thought them into being. It's just that they seemed imminent so I decided I better have a plan. Sometimes I decided not to think about a certain issue until I actually "cross that bridge." I have found success applying both methods of thought. I always want the bottom line. If I know what the bottom line is I can formulate a plan to avoid it or work through it until I've overcome it. *Then I can let go of the worry.* I have also noticed that I do have added resources to help me if I ever am faced with an obstacle that I had worried about for a brief time in the past. In addition, *when I constantly dwell on what I don't want to happen,* I have found it drawn to me with a disturbing power.

Exercise: Think about any recurring thoughts that have feelings of portent or significance. Especially write down anything that seems like a warning.

____

____

____

When you think of these thoughts or feelings do any solutions or guidance accompany them?

____

When worry thoughts play out in your mind take the time to write them down. What is a worry I am currently dealing with?

____

____

____

What is the best-case scenario I could imagine about this coming to resolution?

____

____

What is the worst-case scenario that could happen with this worry?

____

____

____

Write down three actions you could take to prevent the worst-case scenario.

____

____

____

Now imagine or visualize yourself successfully receiving the best-case scenario.

Write down how your feelings changed and the worry dissipated by addressing your concerns and imagining the best outcome.

____

____

____

Exercise: Write down significant experiences that came with premonitions so you can see how they played out. It can be very rewarding to see yourself learning to tune in.

____

____

____

Dreams: Sometimes inspiration or guidance comes in the form of dreams. Dreams can be very significant and have messages for us to understand. I will elaborate more on dreamwork in the chapter

In a literal sense, it was a precursor of an actual event that took place in high school. I went with three friends to go up a hill in a Volkswagen Beetle. The driver was quite proud of his car and was sure it could go up this particular hill without a problem. He was wrong. As the incline increased, the car began to roll down the hill end over end. I remember feeling like everything was in slow motion as we were rolling down the hill. Even with a seatbelt on, we were all severely tossed around in the car. When the car stopped rolling, we were upside down. My head had hit the roof repeatedly and when the car stopped, I was lodged between the front and back seat with my torso. My neck was painfully contorted. Everyone was silent when the car stopped and I remember thinking the others must be dead. Finally, the driver broke the silence and asked if everyone was okay and could we get out of the car. Somehow, we managed to get the doors open and get out.

I remember sitting on the hill a short distance from the car and rocking back and forth—I didn't cry. I was in shock and really scared. The others, two guys and a girl, were crying, especially the driver who was expressing that although he made it through the accident without significant injury, he was afraid his father would be pretty upset when he took the car home. The two guys decided to pick up the car and get it rolled over. I was astounded to see how strong they were as they maneuvered the vehicle and got it turned right side up. At this point, we examined the car for damage. The bumpers were beat up, some paint was scratched, and there was a dent in the car where my head had been slammed against the roof repeatedly. It was visible from the inside and outside of the car. I sustained some significant neck injuries. **It is amazing to me that something so bizarre had been part of my dreams for years.**

Lesson: It is quite worthwhile to develop the ability to remember your dreams. I have learned a technique called _**lucid dreaming**_. I also keep a dream journal in which I record the dreams I remember and my interpretation of them. The symbols in our dreams frequently have valuable meaning for us. Ones that are repeated may have special significance. I have learned to ask the symbols in my dream what they mean and set up sentinels inside my dreams that act as guides and protectors depending on the need. I will elaborate more on this in the

Exercise: When you first wake up think about what you were dreaming.

In the morning keep a dream journal by your bed. Before you open your eyes and lose the memory think of what you were just dreaming about. Now open your eyes and record as much as you can remember about the dream. Record your impressions of the symbolism in your dreams. Check out more information about symbolism in dreams and lucid dreaming. There are books available on the subject. Trust your own interpretation above what you read however

When I have a dream that is significant and has portent for me, it feels different. I know throughout my mind and body that there is something important to be understood from that dream. When I am processing a very difficult issue or past trauma, my subconscious mind works to resolve it for me while I dream. I have had some amazing resolution to trauma in the form of dreams. It's a fascinating subject. See if it feels right for you.

What was your dream about last night?

____

____

Is any of it pertaining to a current problem? What are some solutions offered in the dream?

____

____

____

Experience: I had a bizarre premonition about an event that was not received while I was dreaming. However, it was something that I had thought about repeatedly. I had a freak sewing accident! The women in my family sewed a lot and invariably the pins sometimes ended up in the shag carpet and consequently in the bottom of my foot or someone else's. I had thought about how painful it would be to be crawling on the floor, as I often did while playing with my siblings, and have a pin get jammed into my kneecap. This thought had occurred to me many times and I would look for stray pins before kneeling down on the floor. **The accident scenario was a little different, but I did end up jamming a pin in my knee!**

I had a new dress that was too long for me so I had put it on and was having the hem marked by having pins put in the hemline to make it the proper length. The phone rang and I assumed it would be for me because I was expecting a call from my boyfriend. (This was before cell phones.) As I rushed toward the phone, I hit my knee on the coffee table and drove a two-and-a-half-inch dressmaker pin into my leg just below the kneecap. It broke into several pieces once inside the knee. It required surgery to remove a segment that was a 1/4" long, but the other larger piece was embedded so deeply in the tibia that the doctors decided to leave it in and let in "encapsulate" itself. They concluded that trying to dig it out of the bone would cause too much damage to my leg. Now I had a 4" scar on my knee that was very painful and ugly. I had been competing in beauty pageants before the accident and that was no longer a possibility with a large, elevated, purple scar. In addition, the scar tissue that formed around the scar restricts the proper movement of my kneecap causing pain and lack of mobility, which put an end to my chances for a singing and dancing career, which was a lifelong objective up to that time.

I believe if this had not happened, I wouldn't have become a bodyworker, and I couldn't share my insight with you now.

> **Thoughts and actions can attract negative, harmful experiences, but it is not always the explanation for premonitions.**

Lesson: Some would say that these experiences are indicators of negative self-fulfilling prophecy, but I don't view them that way. I think that having thoughts about, and dreaming about these things beforehand helped to prepare me to handle the event better when it actually happened

Application: If you begin to pay attention, you will instinctively feel which thoughts are simply negativity and which have feelings of portent—something different and more important.

You can then pursue avenues to correct negativity or be prepared for those rare events that are simply inevitable.

Keep a journal of the intuition, promptings, and inspiration you receive. It will give you a way of tracking the frequency and reliability of the things you consider intuition. It will amaze you. It will also give you a map of where you've been and where your intuition leads you. It will be a source of comfort and joy when you feel discouraged because you can see how you are guided and cared for when you tune in properly. It will help to develop your resilience.

Author's Experience: Another example of a very strong premonition occurred shortly after my daughter was born. I began to have the very strong feeling that a loved one was going to die. This was particularly devastating since I was experiencing life threatening health problems at the time and I wondered how I would ever cope with a loved one dying. I felt such despair that I couldn't imagine anything that would be more difficult than a loved one's death at that time. I contemplated it and prayed about it for many months. I was just starting to embark on my healing journey at this time.

Lesson: I learned that visualizing myself handling any difficult situation in advance helps me to behave rationally when I'm faced with the problem in reality.

Because the thought of a loved one's death was so terrifying to me, I mentally rehearsed how I would handle the news and attend the funeral. It turned out that my father was killed in a horrific auto accident, just a few years after this premonition. When my father's death and funeral took place, this advanced preparation allowed me to participate in the memorial program without breaking down emotionally and physically.

His death was completely unexpected. He was on his way home from work and was hit by a car that crossed the centerline, drove into his lane and hit him head on. The other driver's car came up onto the hood of his car and smashed him into the steering wheel and window. He didn't even have time to react. His foot was still on the gas pedal. He was killed instantly and his car and body were severely mangled.

With premonitions, the details sometimes get a little confused for me, but the overall message is the important thing. I thought the impending death was going to be someone else instead of my father at first. I am learning to hone my skills as I go. As I have contemplated my father's death I realize that the mental preparation I did when preparing myself for the possible death of a loved one helped me to cope with the experience of my father's horrifying sudden death, funeral, and burial.

My mother felt a viewing of his body would help our family. What?! It took 3 days of work on his body before the funeral director would allow us to see him. Being around a dead body is one of the worst experiences for me, yet I was able to handle it without becoming frightened or extremely anxious, which is my typical response. He looked good for a body who had been through what he had, but he looked awful compared to his usual self. I was astounded at how well I handled the viewing and the visitation of family members, many of whom wanted to talk about the "bloody" details. It appeared that he had been decapitated and the funeral director was adamant that we not touch his head!

After the funeral, my mother forced me to go to the car he was killed in, to look for some personal things. Despite the horror of the mangled car and his blood all over in the car, I found the strength to lift out and carry around two car doors, by myself, which had been removed and placed in the back of the car. They were heavy enough I don't think I would normally have had the strength to carry them. We are often given added strength in times of crisis. Additionally, I had Adrenal Insufficiency which can make stress cause a life threatening Adrenal Crisis, and I didn't have one!

The premonition allowed me to do the mental work that carried me through the shock of my father's horrible death and subsequent experiences surrounding it.

> **Application: You can learn to rehearse or visualize yourself handling any difficult situation you currently face or may face in the future**

Visualization has endless applications and you will find many suggestions of how to use this fascinating tool to better your life and overcome trauma. Many successful people use visualization to see themselves performing perfectly before the actual planned event takes place. I have heard amazing stories of athletes using visualization to improve their performance and without actually physically practicing, they improved their technique.

The mind has difficulty distinguishing between a real or an imagined event if it's imagined with enough emotion and detail. Visualize yourself acting the way you want to act in a situation that has been difficult for you in the past. If you see it clearly enough and *embody the emotions* you would when you really did it right, you will be able to make this a reality. You can also "reframe" memories. Reframe to me means to change what's already happened by imagining a different outcome, or seeing it from a different perspective in your mind. This is a technique I learned in massage school and have used very successfully to release my own trauma and to facilitate resolution for my clients during somatic/emotional release bodywork.

You can learn to use this to help you accomplish whatever you want.

> **Exercise**: Take a difficult experience you had today or recently that you wish had a different or better outcome. Write it down.
>
> ____
>
> ____

Before you go to bed while you are lying down, visualize yourself experiencing it the way you wished it had gone. Now take several deep cleansing breaths and release the unpleasant image. Now really see yourself in motion experiencing it the way you wish it had gone. This is a way to re-frame difficulty and trauma so the mind and body can let go of it and quit rehearsing it for resolution.

Use your intuition about the suggestions found in this book. Some will resonate with you and you will feel that you should try them out. Other's may have less interest to you but may act as a catalyst propelling you to another idea or source for added information that will be helpful to you.

If you believe that you will receive guidance in how to grow beyond your limitations, you will! I absolutely believe that when you have the single-minded purpose to discover what your limiting beliefs and habits are, they will be revealed to you through the process of intuition, which I have explained.

Your job is to be in tune enough to hear and act on the answer. Since we all have different experiences that shape our thoughts and beliefs, your path of turning your trials into triumphs may vary from mine. *Trust the process* to get the information you need to overcome your difficulties!

Invite God to be a partner and follow your inner voice to know what steps to take to find your life's purpose and achieve your goals.

I have a strong belief in God. I have had many experiences that have revealed God's helping, and vital intervention in my life. I feel a deep and personal relationship with God. My prayers are answered, not always immediately, and sometimes not the way I think they will be, but they are always answered! When I ask for guidance and enlightenment, I get it.

Most of the concepts found in this book are a result of following my intuition, and the answers to prayers. The answers I received guided my healing path and are contained in this book for your benefit.

I recently learned that some of the principles I learned through following this intuition are timeless truths that have been discovered by others throughout history.

Sometimes these truths were carefully guarded and considered too valuable to be shared. I'm always exhilarated when I hear that someone else has received similar insight although we don't know each other and may not even live in the same time in history.

It affirms to me that there are definitely timeless truths that govern the universe and are available to everyone truly seeking. Truth can be received by tuning into your intuition and then taking action when necessary.

Timeless Truth—We Are Not Challenged Above What We Are Able To Bear

I believe in a loving, personal God who is concerned about each of us individually. He won't allow us to be tried above what we can bear or it would be setting us up for failure.

Health

Some of the most difficult problems I have faced in my life have been severe health problems. While I agree that our thoughts and beliefs can greatly influence our health or lack thereof, not all experiences (disease, discomfort) can be transformed by a positive attitude. This may be the primary means of the Divine (God) communicating your lesson to you.

The fact that you experience disease or illness does not necessarily mean you have done something "wrong" or "bad" or you are being punished!

Sometimes an illness is the body's way of communicating to us that something in our thinking or our emotional world is out of balance. It can work for our good when we tune in to our bodies to understand the message it's trying to teach us.

> **When we learn to tell our minds what we want and expect; instead of focusing on what is not working, we can release anger and other emotions stuck in our bodies. Then we can finally free ourselves to heal.**

There are excellent books on the connection between the emotions and our physical health.

For me the key to turning my health around was to tune in, honor my body, and heal the trauma that kept me in turmoil and poor health.

> **Exercise**: Is your body trying to tell you something is out of balance? Use your intuition to find the root cause. Make it a subject of meditation and prayer. Ask yourself out loud, "What is my body trying to tell me that I need to change?"
>
> ____
>
> ____
>
> ____
>
> ____
>
> ____

Use Visualizations to See Yourself Whole and Well

Defining Your Wants and Path Through Visualizations

> **Application: When you "see" yourself achieving all you want to do, be, and have, in your mind, you have set in motion the powers that will bring it to you.**

Many authors have written about the power of visualization. My introduction to it came in massage school from an instructor who was trained in Neuro-Linguistic Programming and then again in a workshop for bodyworkers to learn to release trauma from their clients.

The concept is you can change your reality, your trauma and your perceptions by what you vividly imagine with emotion. You can create a new reality. Whatever you want to see in reality, see it first in your mind.

Take time each day to relax, close your eyes, take a few deep cleansing breaths and focus all of your energy and intensity on seeing what you want in your life. Imagine all the details you can about what you want to experience in reality. How will it taste, feel, smell, and sound to experience what you want. Imagine it with as much emotion as you can create. You will be communicating this direction to your subconscious mind, which processes information mostly in images and feelings.

When your subconscious mind understands what you want with clarity and concise emotion and detail, you can draw it to you with a force that will astound you. It must be a daily habit to be the most effective. Spend daily quality time developing your thoughts to reap the greatest rewards. Instead of imagining your limitations, **think and act in your visualization as though anything positive can happen to you.** (This can feel like a real stretch of the imagination at first depending on how much trauma you have experienced.)

Examples of things to visualize: Think abundance instead of lack and you will see it in your outer reality. Perhaps you need to imagine assertively confronting someone and feeling perfectly calm while doing it and then resolving the problem effectively. Perhaps you need to see yourself having the perfect job interview and working at the company of your choice for the salary of your choice.

Every time you start to feel depressed, you might need to imagine that you are feeling very happy doing an activity that delights you in an exotic destination. Perhaps you need to imagine that every cell of your body is healthy and functioning perfectly, or that you have a trim, athletic body instead of the one you now occupy. You can think yourself thin. I have found it helpful to take old photographs of myself at my ideal weight and every morning and night look at them and say to myself. "This is me!" I am becoming thinner everyday until I reach my ideal weight." So far, I have lost 15 pounds without dieting using these visual cues and visualizing how it feels to be thin again. It's pretty exciting. Whatever you want, visualization is a powerful tool to bring it about. Try it!

Stop Making Excuses

No matter how difficult and traumatic your history, with the help of God, your own sheer tenacity, and a willingness to take personal responsibility for your own actions and not enable other's bad behavior, you will overcome the trauma and reclaim your life. You can enjoy the peace, prosperity, and joy you are designed to experience if you will implement the right actions and persevere. I believe this with all my heart because I have not shared my most traumatic experiences in this book, but they help me to know that you can make it through and triumph over anything!

> **Someday we have to quit blaming our history and stand up and be accountable for our own thoughts, problems, and behaviors.**

There is so much awareness and information available to teach us how to overcome our struggles and makes positive changes. It really takes away all our excuses, so make a change!

Jenny's Story: "I have been subjected to extreme forms of physical and emotional abuse and assaults that wounded my body and scarred my mind. As a child, I was subjected to people who abused me in every conceivable way. When I took a class on self-defense to learn to fight all my "ghosts"—the memories of abuse and assault resurfaced. It was the beginning of my journey to reclaim my life and body. Everyone cheered for me as I fought through my flashbacks and successfully defended myself and graduated from my self-defense class.

Mental abuse seems particularly heinous to me. I feel like I will eventually heal from the physical damage but the emotional abuse was much more insidious. What the abusers said and the way they worked to control my thoughts and behaviors has stayed in my mind and affected every thought, behavior, and decision I make. These horrible and terrifying experiences combined to form a pretty bleak outlook on life, but I just kept trying harder and harder to get out of the trap.

I used to be confused by the abusers always insisting that everything is really all my fault. I have turned myself inside out trying to please and placate them. My changes and efforts never changed their behavior toward me. The abusers always kept me guessing. What was acceptable one day could be the reason for a dramatic outburst of anger and punishment the next."

Tracy shared this experience with me:" I remember my grandmother always screaming at my grandfather for things. If he forgot to put out the trash, she'd dump it out down the stairs for him to pick up. If he left his clothes lying around she'd throw them out the window. She was okay most of the time, except when she'd been drinking. I remember them fighting once when I was there and my grandmother threw a knife, which landed in my grandfather's abdomen. It required surgery, yet my grandfather wouldn't admit how he got a knife in the belly to anyone. He left for several months but he came back."

Lesson: Many people have a pattern of seeking out relationships and circumstances that continue the victimization cycle even though they want desperately to be free from abuse. Contrary, to popular opinion, they are not some type of masochist who secretly desires to be treated with violence and contempt because they get some type of gratification from it. Both men and women can be involved in emotionally and physically destructive relationships.

Exercise: Write down the answers to these questions. Think very carefully about the situations in your life that have caused or are currently causing you to feel the most distress. Is there any pattern that you recognize?

____

____

____

Does the situation always happen repeatedly at a certain time of year, or after a certain stimulus? (Are you stuck in an "anniversary" pattern?

____

____

____

Can you identify who else or what else made you feel this way? (What is the origin?)

____

____

____

____

Lesson: The abuse perpetrator is not the *entire problem*. What you do with the experiences determines your level of happiness and achievement. Each person involved has a part in the problem of abuse. This is not to say I blame the victim. I do not condone abuse, but once a victim learns other options of behaving and thinking the abuse can't happen anymore!

Application: Sometimes what we think is the worst possible thing that could happen turns out to be the greatest benefit if we use it to think of new ways of relating, or can learn to recognize the lesson learned in the crisis. Try to learn to see the lesson while you're still in the crisis. It will shorten the time of crisis.

Author's Experience: Being disowned was painful, yet it provided a crucial break from the incredible control that was exerted upon me throughout my relationship with my parents. The divorce allowed me to be free from a caustic relationship. It was very powerful and liberating.

Application: Once you break free from all toxic relationships, your thoughts, habits, and behaviors can change dramatically. As long as you continue in them, you cannot effectively change. The abusers do not want you to change. And will do all they can to keep you in old patterns of relating to each other.

Author's History: I could say that the dominant feeling in my life up until a decade ago has been pain--emotional, physical and spiritual. I had a painful hernia that required surgery when I was just six weeks old and weighed less that 10 pounds. As my life progressed, I found myself continuously involved in deeply painful situations.

Some people think that we don't remember our early life experiences but my work as a licensed massage therapist and bodyworker suggests a very different view. We remember all of our experiences—they become embedded in our bodies and cells. The most painful ones are often stored in our subconscious mind far beyond our conscious memory, but they can deeply affect our lives and our choices.

Author's Experience: When I was a young child my mother says I was hyperactive. I was never medicated for it but I remember that I literally climbed the walls. I would get into the doorframe and shimmy up to the top but would not be able to get down. I had a terrible time trying to hold still and pay attention for more than a few minutes at a time. (Could it be that I always wanted to get away? Hmmmmm.)

My father would set me on top of the refrigerator and tell me he would let me down if I could hold still for one minute. I never could and I ended up spending too much time on top of the refrigerator--a most unpleasant experience. This was an experience that contributed to my fear of heights. **The other would be him holding me over a very steep cliff pretending to throw me off the side (Dead Horse Point) and many other very high places.** Despite this difficulty with concentration, I excelled in school and rose to the top of the class in junior high through college. It was a constant effort to channel the energy effectively. These are the things I learned to help me along the way.

Lesson: I learned to get up and move to work off the need to "wiggle" all the time. I learned to pace myself in all my activities including work, and studying. I would get up to do another activity every few hours. The diversion refreshed my mind and I could come back to my previous activities with renewed interest and creativity.

Before studying, it helped to do a physical activity that engaged all the hemispheres of my brain. I like cross crawl patterning (left hand on right knee then right hand on left knee, repeated for several minutes) to get maximum comprehension. Even as an adult I found my attention waning and my concentration disturbed if I didn't take a break frequently. I had enough energy for several people and could accomplish many tasks in about half the time it took others to do the same.

Gradually, I learned to work with the energy through exercise and diversion tactics. About the time I learned how to cope with my enormous energy I suffered from a terminal illness and had the energy of a slug! After an incredible struggle I've overcome that also. These experiences have helped me learn to use my mind and attention much more efficiently.

Exercise: What habits, attitudes, or self-defeating behaviors would you like to overcome? List as many as you can think of now. ____ ____ ____ ____ ____ ____ ____ As you continue through this book, you will develop a personal plan of how to achieve them based on suggestions found in this book. The more creative you get in your solutions, the more likely you are to succeed. Involving all your senses will anchor your new solutions into your subconscious most effectively.

Author's Experience: I developed quite early physically. By the time I was eleven, I was attracting a lot of unwanted sexual attention. As I grew, the number and intensity of inappropriate responses from people increased. Several educators pursued me sexually. Total strangers often physically and verbally accosted me. They'd say how they wanted a piece of me or make obscene sexual gestures.

Some were bold enough to grope me in public. I'd be standing in a crowd and someone would grab my butt or touch my breasts. I would never be able to determine exactly who did it. More than once I was threatened with rape.

I had a series of severe back injuries and began swimming regularly at a local hotel to rehabilitate and strengthen my back. (The hotel had the only indoor pool in town.) At least once a week I was invited by a stranger to come up to his room for sex. I was still a minor. Some would try to give me their hotel keys. I got a lot of inappropriate comments about how great I looked swimming and then they would elucidate on how they felt about my body.

Some dates, acquaintances, and even strangers would tell me how they could "take it from me if I wouldn't put out." I was propositioned constantly in the most vulgar terms. Men followed me around the campus at the university I attended and would not even bother to ask me out. They'd just say, "Let's go F***". I was not remotely flattered. I once had a date tell me he was going to rape me as he pinned me to the couch he said, "You'd chew your arm off to get away wouldn't you?" I had to fight like hell and he finally let me go.

Lesson: Everyone has to learn to set boundaries, emotionally, physically and spiritually. I had to give myself permission to stand up for myself even if that meant I wasn't liked or it offended someone. I had to learn that anyone invading your personal space with force—whether emotionally or physically—needs to be told "No!" I slowly learned I had a right to my own thoughts and feelings and that I could disagree with someone and still be okay. (This took some effort because disagreeing in the past provoked death threats.)

In self-defense classes I learned my "tough walk", my "don't fuss with me" physical stance, and how to use my voice forcefully to set boundaries. When I started doing this my life began to change drastically and suddenly I felt like I had a little control over what happened to me in my life.

<table>
<tr><td>

Exercise: Think of a circumstance or a person that you habitually have problems with. Do you have anyone in your life who always seems to get the upper hand with you. Do you have a boss, co-worker, or an acquaintance who get their way through yelling, swearing, intimidation, or demeaning you? Would you like that relationship to be different? Are there things you wish you could say to them but just don't have the nerve? How do you anticipate you would feel if you could effectively express your point of view? Write your answers here.

____

____

____

____

____

____

</td></tr>
</table>

With a supportive friend, try role-playing effective communication and assertiveness techniques that would assist you next time you are with the person you have difficulty with. Try visualizing yourself feeling calm and assertive and handling the situation in an ideal manner. It will be far more likely to happen with this type of advanced preparation.

Author's Experience: During my life I developed a large number of health problems. Since it's estimated that around 90% of all illness is stress related, I can reasonably assume that all of the stress in my life played a large role in the development of these serious illnesses.

I began developing severe food and environmental allergies that would cause anaphylactic reactions by the age of 12. The symptoms were that my throat would itch and begin swelling shut, and my face would swell and I had terrible abdominal cramping. It was frightening, painful, and life threatening. I was finally reduced to about 15 foods I could eat without a severe reaction. I took all of the allergy treatments available at the time. I had to cook all of my food from scratch and eat a rotation diet that didn't allow me to eat the same food sooner than four days after the last time I ate it. It was incredibly time consuming and frustrating.

I developed ulcerative colitis that caused severe pain and bleeding. It was activated each time I experienced emotional distress. I spent years of continuous bleeding despite drastic measures to treat it with cortisone treatments.

I have had 21 incredibly painful kidney stones and developed a life-threatening illness as a result of being in chronic fight or flight mode (Adrenal Insufficiency).

Lesson: As I began to deal with the root causes of my difficult experiences, and my emotions about them, the allergies began to clear. Eventually I have been able to eradicate allergies from my life. Nearly all my health problems had a root in trauma—mostly feelings and habits of thought and my responses to them. I have now eliminated the kidney stones, adrenal insufficiency, and eliminated with the ulcers. But there was more for me to overcome!

Author's Experience: My own challenges with severe health problems have tested my mettle and helped me to understand how our indomitable will to heal can carry us through any situation.

I wanted very much to have children. It was incredibly difficult for me to carry a child to term. I had seven miscarriages before I could bear a child. Even the successful pregnancy was fraught with extreme difficulty. I had to have hormone therapy to maintain the pregnancy. I developed gestational diabetes and had to take large amounts of insulin in shots as often as six times a day. When that didn't control the blood sugar I had to be hospitalized and became a human pincushion with all of the blood sugar monitoring and insulin shots that increased to about every three hours.

I had pre-term labor from about the sixteenth week, which severely restricted my work as a massage therapist and all other activities. Eventually it caused me to have doctor-ordered complete and total bed-rest for the last two months. As the pregnancy progressed, the placenta began deteriorating and jeopardized the life of my child. I had to be induced to bear the child **six weeks early** because of severe complications in my body. Fortunately, she had complete lung development.

I can only say, it was the birth was like hell! I will spare you the bloody details. We both almost died. I watched my daughter be resuscitated because she had no heartbeat and was not breathing when they finally got her out. (It took six people working on me and in me simultaneously to get her out.) Her face was blue and so distorted that one eye was an inch lower than the other. I remember thinking, "How could this happen after I've lost seven other babies? If she lives, she is so disfigured that she will be ridiculed and embarrassed all her life. What chances will she have at any semblance of a normal life? And simultaneously thinking, "God if she dies you may as well take me too because I can't take anymore of this!" The nurse quickly placed her in my arms so we could bond very briefly and then rushed her to the special care unit where she stayed for several days.

After my daughter was born, I became extremely ill with post-partum toxemia and other severe problems. Without any insulin, my blood sugar dropped to levels that could cause coma on several occasions. (**Normal blood sugar levels are 80 to 130. I got down**

to 32 and was miraculously coherent enough to be able to take a blood sample. I should have been unconscious or dead.) I was eating constantly but could not maintain high enough blood sugar levels to do any of my normal activities. I was incredibly weak, shaky, and had difficulty concentrating. I felt like I was going to die. I went for some extensive testing where the doctor tested me for a brain tumor and a pancreas tumor among other things. I was only 30 years old and now that I had borne a child, it looked as if I wouldn't be alive to raise her and my beautiful son whom we had adopted. I was finally tested for an endocrine disease.

While the test was being administered, one nurse casually announced to the other that one of their patients had died the night before. I said that was unfortunate, and asked how old she was. The nurse said, "She wasn't very old but she was really sick." She died from the illness I was being tested for! I was very upset to learn that I too had the illness she died from!

So began the fight for my life against adrenal insufficiency, a disease that has affected every facet of my life. My body was unable to deal with stress properly and ordinary illnesses became life threatening. I experienced symptoms of extreme fatigue, lowered immune response, severe hypoglycemia, weakness, trembling, nausea, and vomiting. As these and other symptoms progress in a crisis, the circulatory system collapses and causes death, usually from heart failure.

This disease is greatly aggravated by stress. It was hard for me to deal with stress from illness or emotional distress without shaking and experiencing many of the symptoms described. My past traumas from a lifetime of fight or flight hormone overproduction caused the adrenal glands to fail.

Here is one of my experiences that helped me make it through when I just didn't think had the strength. The stress of filing for divorce sent me into several months of adrenal crises. I really felt like giving up and dying. During one episode, I was weak and shaky, my heart was beating irregularly, and I was vomiting. I felt I was going to die before the night ended. I called my children and sister to me and expressed my love for them. I told them that I might not be with them very long, but I knew somehow that the Lord would care for them. I had discussed with her that I didn't want my children to be traumatized by dying in front of them or by them finding my dead body in the morning. I felt they were too young to handle that. My sister took my children to her apartment so that I could be alone. My sister told me that my son collapsed on her stairs and began sobbing, "I don't want my mommy to die!" He started praying for me. I began feeling better some hours later because they were all praying for me. I called her and she brought the children back. **I am certain that without their faith and prayers that my life would have ended that night.**

This episode was the beginning of several months that could only be described as **hell** in which I sought medical treatment to no avail. I ended up in the emergency room with heart pain. The doctor said that I must not be having a heart attack because I was laughing. I told him it was my way of dealing with all the trauma in my life. I was diagnosed with pericarditis, inflammation of the heart. I think I was dying of a broken heart among other things. After repeated adrenal crises, I was finally able to get a second medical opinion. I went with a list of my symptoms and explained how I was fighting through the rigors of death too frequently. He said, "We have done all we can for you and I'm releasing you to your primary care physician." He sent me home to die. I thought it was the end, because I was being abandoned by the medical profession to die. Surely it couldn't get any worse.

It wasn't the end, and it actually got worse!

My devoted sister who had cared for me extensively during this time of crisis now had to move to another state because her husband's job was eliminated. Now I was completely on my own with no relative in the state. I didn't have any idea how I would handle two young children, deal with the aftermath of a divorce, and be well enough to support us alone. I fought death with everything in me because I wanted to be alive to raise my children. I had to learn to stand on my own in a hurry.

During this time of illness after I had filed for divorce, I learned what poverty felt like. I was too ill to work. I had to rely on the aid from others who helped support me by paying some of my bills and provided me with food. It was very difficult to accept the help because I wanted to be independent. It was a time of great humility for me. I had to accept the help because I had no choices.

Although I am extremely grateful for all the assistance, I determined that I will never be in that situation again! It was so limiting. I can understand why poverty is such a difficult condition having experienced it along with severe health problems simultaneously. My divorce took a long time to be finalized. It became very costly, and I had to sell my home to pay the legal fees.

Lesson: When I had to sell my home I felt it was wrenched away from me. Now I realize that selling my home allowed me to pay off all my debt, legal fees, and to cut ties with people who were not emotionally supportive to me. After I left the area where I lived before, I felt stronger than I ever had in my life. I felt free to think, and reason, and act in the best interest of my children and myself. **I learned that I had more fortitude and personal strength than I ever could have imagined having.** Since that time, I learned through enormous effort some things that helped to improve my life tremendously. My physical health has greatly increased and I am able to work again and find satisfaction in doing so.

> **Application: When you have learned the lesson that your experiences are working to teach you, you will receive a reward for your efforts.** You will experience the joy of having some resolution of the difficulty. You will find the peace and joy you seek. You will gain a trust in your ability to handle crises and feel inner strength. These are priceless!

Author's Experience: Taking Stock:

I had reached a point when my life was intolerable. For some of us it takes hitting rock bottom to say "enough is enough!" I took a careful accounting of my personality characteristics and traits to determine which ones were working and which I must discard. I liked that I was innately cheerful despite incredibly difficult circumstances. I have a spontaneous laugh that fills a room and people are attracted to me because they like how they feel when they are with me. I like my deep and overwhelming desire for knowledge because it drives me to find solutions to my problems and makes life far more rewarding.

I have been blessed with many talents, I sing, dance well, and enjoy working with my hands such as embroidery, painting, and giving massages. I have developed skills within massage that have caused many people to say it was the best massage they have ever had. I love people and have an easy manner that makes me approachable. I love to perform through speaking, singing, and music and dance. A professor of Psychology once told me that I was the only true extrovert he had ever met. I feel I am a very compassionate person and sense the needs and feelings of others. I believe I am an especially sensitive and caring mother. I like all of these things about me and they work for me.

Now some might take this assessment as conceit but in order to move forward and claim our best possible life we have to acknowledge the things we like about ourselves and what's working before we beat ourselves up emotionally for what we don't like about ourselves and what's not working.

<table>
<tr><td>Exercise: List as many of your talents, attributes and good qualities you can think of. Then acknowledge that you really are fabulous.

</td></tr>
</table>

What wasn't working: One of the things that I didn't like was the inability to effectively stand up for myself when someone was invading my territory physically or emotionally. This created a lot of inner turmoil and hardship. I was constantly in situations that gave me opportunities to stand up for myself but I rarely did.

An example of this occurred when I was a teenager. We had a neighbor who just moved into the neighborhood. She was younger than I was but my parents insisted I befriend her. She had been living in a foreign country where she was allowed to spit on people she considered inferior. She was very competitive with me and wanted complete control over the relationship with my best friend of four years, who was also a neighbor. On the bus, at school, and walking home she would spit "snot globs" in my hair and on my beautiful coat. I tried to avoid her but I couldn't seem to and when I discussed it with my parents, they insisted that I continue to interact with her and be her friend. I was instructed to include her in my friendships and activities.

I was so concerned about displeasing my parents and being punished by them for disobeying, that I allowed her to treat me with total contempt. Inwardly I wanted to defend myself forcibly, but I refrained. Once she physically attacked me, scratching and kicking me, in my own yard, simply because she knew I would not stand up for myself. It was horrible!

I wanted to be assertive yet whenever I acted in an assertive manner it created serious anxiety because I had such a high need to please others. I had a higher need to keep the peace and minimize conflicts wherever they occurred, than I did to be treated with respect and have my thoughts and feelings validated. I was baffled as to why I couldn't stand up for myself.

> **One of the most powerful things you can say to others who criticize you is: "I'm not invested in your opinion of me!"**

I had the opportunity to say this to an ecclesiastical leader who was chastising me for not including a belligerent and toxic person in a special event I was holding to honor my son's achievement as Eagle Scout. When I said it if felt like the most powerful thing I've ever said and I have used it as an affirmation to remind me that I don't have to please everyone. I have to live true to MY value system. Try it, you'll like it!

> **Exercise:** What areas in your life do you need to stand up for yourself and set some boundaries?
>
> ____
>
> ____

Commit to yourself to speak your truth and set appropriate boundaries regardless of the cost or how unpopular it makes you.

Negative Self-Talk

> **Exercise:** Take a minute to write down the words you hear in your head and say to yourself about yourself. What do you hear when you mess up and do something you regret?

> _______________________________
> _______________________________
> _______________________________
>
> **Can you see a pattern in how you perform based on what you say to yourself?**
> Write down your self-fulfilling prophecies, i.e., "I always say the wrong thing." Or "I
> always screw up and ruin people's lives." What you say to yourself comes about.
>
> _______________________________
> _______________________________
> _______________________________

Another trait that I had was continually berating myself. I had internalized the opinions and labels of those people who were the most unkind to me, not the ones who were my true friends. I began analyzing my interactions with the people I had the most trouble with and came up with some definite common denominators. I realized that I played out a similar pattern of victimization and passiveness with each of the people I felt the worst around. I knew I had to change.

One of the consequences of this passive behavior was I lost my singing voice. The three octaves of power I once enjoyed with singing shrunk to about 5 notes. I was devastated. I had always defined myself by my ability to sing. "I was a singer" foremost. As I pondered, prayed, and meditated on this problem, it came to me that I had lost my ability to sing because it was a symbolic representation of a larger problem in my life. Singing gave me such joy, and I was not feeling any joy at that time in my life and I felt **"I had no voice"** in what was happening in my life. I had refused to make my voice heard and stand up for myself in a myriad of situations and the problem manifested itself by the loss of my voice.

In order to regain my singing voice, I had to become assertive and "voice my opinions, voice my emotions, and voice my need for change." When I began to do this, my voice gradually returned but I went for almost five years without being able to sing.

When I am having bodywork to release trauma, I have to **"give it a voice"** or name the trauma or what happened aloud in order to resolve and release the trauma. Giving myself back "a voice" has been a powerful source of healing for me.

> **Exercise**: Is there an area in your life where you are holding back from speaking your truth or setting a boundary that you need to be healthy and happy? Write down something you need to "give a voice."
>
> _______________________________
> _______________________________
> _______________________________

Jenny expressed a similar problem. She says, "It seemed like every situation I encountered was one in which I assumed the role of a victim. I felt immense shame, because I didn't stand up for myself. My passive behavior allowed others to take severe advantage of me. I felt hopelessness at times and guilty because I felt that I was expected to turn the other cheek and endure whatever people did to me because I wanted to be a good Christian.

It created a terrible internal conflict that was destroying my emotional health. I also felt fearful for my safety. Because I have been assaulted several times, I was so afraid that it would never stop and I would continue to be hurt all the time."

> **Application: It is obvious from Jenny's experiences, my own experiences, and those of many others that we become stuck in perpetual cycles.**

These can be positive cycles where we are constantly receiving good things and experiences, but too often, it is a negative cycle. This is very prevalent with abuse victims.

> **Move yourself out of perpetual negative cycles.**

It has been well documented that people who have been sexually assaulted as a child are often the victim of rape and other forms of assault throughout their lives.

This is because the normal healthy boundaries have been violated and the person blocks out a lot of information available to them about their environment because it feels better or safer. This is often called "dissociation." A victim will shut off awareness of their body and their environment as a means of coping with the previous violation. They feel betrayed by their body for letting them be victimized in the first place so they deny their feelings and withdraw from their body.

If you ask victims of sexual assault "Where do you live in your body?," they will most often point to their heads. To themselves they are alive only in their minds. They have disconnected from the body that hurts, and experienced rape and assault. Unfortunately, because they spend most of their time, "spaced out" they are easy prey for predators of all types.

Before they realize it, they are assaulted again because they are disconnected from their bodies and environments or they have minimized the danger or motives of another person as a coping device. When the actual assault takes place they often "freeze" with fear or become very passive because it has become a conditioned response. Their thinking is, "If I couldn't stop a rape the first time, what good would it do to fight this time." **This cycle of psychic numbness produces greater vulnerability to more traumas and more assault.**

Negative Perpetuating Cycles

I was living out ever perpetuating cycles in the most negative sense.

Author's Experience: One of the powerful ways this was manifested to me was in the customers who showed up for bodywork/massage when I was feeling frightened, vulnerable, or powerless. It was as if a magnetic attraction had brought them to my business where the negative drama unfolded repeatedly. Here are several examples to illustrate this point.

I had a man come looking for sexual favors and I didn't know how to respond effectively at first. I could tell when he first came in that I was going to have a problem with him. On his intake form he was "Mr. Anonymous." He had no address just a P.O. Box, no phone number, no employer, no emergency contact person, and he would not meet my gaze. Although he did not state his intentions at first, they became quite obvious as the massage progressed.

As we got started with the massage, he started saying some pretty strange things, like "Can you dig your fingernails into my buttocks?" and he kept exposing his butt. I remained silent and just covered him back up. Then he reached down to stroke my calf. I jerked it away and became very angry, but still said nothing fearing that if I did it would be too confrontational. **Finally, he reached up to touch my breasts. I moved his hands and asked him to get dressed and leave**! He got dressed and came out of the treatment room, *but refused to leave.* I had to physically escort him to the door. I could not believe anyone would be so brazen as to act that way.

Another client came, who grilled me for about 45 minutes about how safe I was in giving massages, and could I really defend myself, and what would I do if I was attacked? I was very frightened but as usual continued to massage him and minimize the danger in my own mind.

The next time he came, he told me he wanted to bring a gun into my office. I told him absolutely not—he would have to leave it in his car. He was now trying to intimidate me with firearms, because I had been too passive in my response to his initial harassment about my safety. *This time I drew the line and called his referring doctor and told him I would not be treating this client any longer.*

The next and strangest experience occurred when I was treating a client for a prescribed series of injury massage treatments lasting several months. He was overly friendly and called me "honey, dear, sweetie, etc." I told him I was uncomfortable with it, but he continued. Unfortunately, I was not firm enough in my convictions to quit treating him yet. As usual, things escalated.

One day he came in for a treatment and decided to do a little dance on my mind. He started talking to me about his sexual conquests, which I asked him to stop talking about. **So he switched gears and started talking to me about all of the people he had assaulted!** He told me in detail how he had taken a broken bottle and nearly torn off the nose of a man. **He had absolutely no way of knowing that I knew the guy whose face he had "re-arranged." He was also a client.** (His face was very scarred and his nose was severely displaced.)

Now I was scared! He could feel it even though I was trying to act tough. Next, he started talking about all of his **occult powers** and activities. Now he had crossed a line I don't let anyone cross. He told me he could control the elements. **I was trying to think of a way to tell him to leave when lightning struck in the pasture just behind our yard!**

It hit with such force that I thought the window of the treatment room was going to break out so I reflexively starting bolting for the door. I grabbed his hand to help him out so he wouldn't be hit by flying glass. He got up off the table and wrapped himself around my body.

He was so pleased with himself because he had been working up to this for months. He was all over me. I asked him to get dressed and leave. Next, I called his referring doctor and asked him not to send anyone else that he wouldn't want in his home alone with his wife! I still wonder to this day if the lightening was coincidental or a real manifestation of his claimed occult powers. **If I had only told him I wouldn't treat him anymore when he started acting inappropriately, I could have prevented myself some substantial fear.**

Learn to set clear emotional and physical boundaries.

Lesson: I was unwilling to feel afraid like this any longer so I took several self-defense classes. I learned to set clear emotional and physical boundaries. I also experienced the feel of how much force it required to deliver a knockout blow. I rehearsed many different assault scenarios with techniques specific to each situation and felt confident that I could now defend myself, physically and verbally.

Probably the most important thing I learned was to take charge of the situation before it escalated, and to quit discounting my intuition about danger and minimizing the inappropriate actions of others. It was so empowering! I have spent many years now in the study of martial arts. The knowledge, skills and attitudes I have acquired through this study have been enormously helpful and have changed the way people interact with me. I receive much more respect.

At that time I didn't know I had the right to refuse the customer service when he didn't provide me with the information required on my intake form. Many years later after these three frightening experiences occurred, I consulted an attorney about it. She informed me that any unwanted touch or just the threat of unwanted touch was illegal and inappropriate. I could refuse service to anyone. Now I include this particular fact – my right of refusal – in my health intake forms.

With my new skills and attitudes I am willing to risk offending someone by pointing out their behavior is offensive to me instead of letting things escalate to the levels they have in the past.

WHEN I SAW THIS REPEATING PATTERN HAPPEN SO FREQUENTLY IN MANY DIFFERENT SETTINGS, I REALIZED I WAS LIVING OUT AN UNSEEN POWER OF ATTRACTION IN THE MOST NEGATIVE SENSE.

Author's Experience: My whole life has been spent trying to figure out how to change what was happening to me so I could be safe and feel joy. I spend a lot of time analyzing how my actions might be received or are actually received by others. If my actions give me the desired outcome I continue. If I get a negative outcome, I change my strategy.

I'm very invested in not giving up my personal power to someone who is abusing his or her power or authority. *I have been reasoning this way since I was two years old.*

Seeing this negative pattern, I reasoned that if I could attract such negativity through my fears, surely I could attract positive experiences by letting go of fear and developing new habits of thought and ways of reacting. When I began to act on this new idea I began to make powerful changes. I developed the skill of turning various situations around in my mind and trying out new behaviors until I began getting my desired outcome.

> **You can change the things you attract to yourself by changing your thoughts and behaviors.**

> **Application: Because I recognized a pattern of passiveness and victimization in myself, I knew I had to change my pattern of relating to people.** This was definitely a characteristic I had to discard. After a careful evaluation of characteristics in my personality that were not working, I conscientiously "blew up" my passive personality and started over.

I erased many of the major characteristics of my personality. I sculpted each day and chiseled away at the old and dysfunctional ways of thinking and behaving until I was living and thinking in more productive and helpful ways.

> **Begin sculpting the work of art that will become the new you.**

One of the first truths I had to recognize was that I had a right to be treated with respect by others. I had to realize that my feelings and needs were as valid and important as the next person. I especially had to learn that I had the right to protest unfair or abusive treatment from others regardless of whether the abuse was emotional or physical. Inside I always knew these things but I had been forced to deny my needs and rights to many abusive people as I grew up.

It took tremendous effort to acknowledge my rights and stand up for them. When I had done this as a child the retaliatory results were often unbearable resulting in many injuries. I still live with a certain amount of fear of retaliation from the abusive people still in the periphery of my life.

Each day is an exercise of choosing faith and personal power over fear. I learned to embrace the concept that it really is unacceptable for others to violate my personal boundaries whether the boundaries are emotional or physical. It is not just about my "opinions" differing from the offenders. I would often hear "It's only YOUR opinion that I'm being abusive.**" The truth is the other person's rights end where mine begin, especially when it comes to my body!**

I made other dynamic changes. Being a "healer/fixer" personality, I sometimes took on responsibilities that should not have been mine. I quit taking responsibility for other peoples' bad behavior and insisted that they take responsibility for it themselves. This was frequently an unpopular move. The abusive people in my life tried to force me to "change back" to taking their abuse.

Exercise: Think of a problem or a pattern in your relationships or in your work environment that keeps recurring. Write it down. (Example, "I keep finding partners who act just like my mother or father." Or "I keep taking jobs that are dissatisfying and people undervalue me or mistreat me.")

____

____

____

What feelings can you identify that contribute to this pattern?

____

____

What one belief or thought could you change that would help you to attract or live out what your really want?

____

____

Self Defense:

I teach others how to forcefully set boundaries with their voice and their posture in ways that deter threatening people and situations.

I have used my voice setting boundaries to keep a man from entering my car when he was trying to enter it on 2 different occasions in different places! Once while I was getting back into my car after using a bank ATM, and another time while I was at a stoplight but had my window rolled down because my air conditioner was broken. I only rolled down the back window to be safer but he crossed 3 lanes of traffic and had his torso through my back window when I yelled at him to "Get the Hell out of my car NOW!"

My voice and posture were so intimidating they both backed up without needing to use any weapons at all!

Take a self-defense class. *It helps you get in touch with your body and overcome passiveness and fearfulness about your ability to defend yourself. I believe that every female needs to know how to defend herself from an unwanted attack.*

Releasing Anger

Author's Experience: Probably the most crucial factor in my healing was that I allowed myself the space and time to get angry about the events of my life that I felt the most traumatized by. I had never done this before because I was truly afraid that if I tapped into the anger I felt from the trauma I had experienced, it would consume me and I would never recover. I always felt before this time that anger was destructive no matter what its cause or justification, and that I could not afford to let myself get out of the rigid control I maintained over my anger. I didn't want to act like the people who had used their rage against me. Because of environmental conditioning, I had learned to stuff my feelings, especially anger, just to survive.

Lesson: What I learned was that anger is an emotion that is often elicited by the fight or flight response and can be a strong stimulus to help us take needed action. I finally learned that siphoning off the anger was a much more healthy and productive response than trying to ignore it and making myself sick.

I also talked with a friend who was going through some rage therapy where her counselor actually encouraged her to connect with and create some anger about the violations that she had experienced. He had her scream and hit things with a padded bat. I bought myself a punching bag and gloves, and when I felt totally frustrated or angry, I punched out the anger in an acceptable way on the punching bag. I also did some screaming into my pillow.

Another friend suggested that "journaling" could be a great healthy release for all the emotions and experiences you need to get out of your body and let go of. She suggested that I write down in my own handwriting rather than on a computer the specific trauma, and feelings I had about it, each night before I went to bed. Then in the morning read it again and destroy it. I found that tearing it up and **watching it burn** was very cleansing to me. I have found this "journaling" technique to be extremely valuable.

These techniques worked well for me because I needed to express my anger. The anger was left in my body until I acknowledged it. The unresolved anger had caused substantial deterioration of my physical health until I used these techniques.

Caution! If you are a "rage addict"-- meaning someone who rages reactively to trivial events and destroys relationships with your actions and words, or you have assaulted people in a rage, then getting in touch with your anger is going to be counter-productive and possibly dangerous. Please seek anger management groups as they have a record of being transformational, much like anonymous groups for other addicts. Rage addicts need professional help.

Lesson: It was hard but with persistence, I completely released my passive behavior. I replaced it with confident, assertive behavior. I made a model of myself that was strong, confident, and functional. I liked who I was becoming. I continue to work at it daily. The huge changes I made were less painful than the way I had been living for the previous decades!

Exercise: Practice journaling to liberate your feelings and to diffuse anger. What experiences have you had that still stir up anger when you think about them?

What do you wish you could have said or done? Write down what you would like to say to the perpetrator or antagonist in the situation. Hold nothing back.

You may want to expand on this by imagining reading a letter of what you wish you could have said to your antagonist as if they were sitting in front of you and had to listen. After reading the letter burn it and feel all the rage dissipate from your body and leave your mind. Now say aloud "And now it is finished! I am free!"

Buy a punching bag and use it. Use assertive communication to set boundaries with people who invade your emotional and physical space.

I have Affirmations for Transforming Anger in the Appendix of this book.

Practice Positive Self-Talk

Learn to talk kindly to yourself and others. Tune in to your thoughts frequently and when you catch yourself berating your actions or thoughts, back up and say it again to yourself in a loving and encouraging way.

When you find yourself repeatedly rehearsing something that was difficult or hurtful say to yourself," That's over now, it has no power over me!" Refuse to replay old dysfunctional messages in your mind. When one begins to surface say, "I am in control of my thoughts." Or say, "Stop the thought" and replace it with a more empowering one.

Learn the Difference Between Passive, Assertive, and Aggressive Behavior

> "The most powerful people in the world are those who choose to control themselves and limit the manipulative power of others toward them."—Phoenix

Application: Make your interactions with other people experiences where you are assertive and proactive—meaning you go after what you want and meet your own needs. Be respectful of the feelings of others but don't give up important personal needs just to appease others. I have raised my children by how I wanted to be treated—virtually the opposite of what I actually experienced. When others needs and wants differ from mine I ask myself, "Is there anything inherently harmful in what they want from me?" and "What part of this request am I willing and able to meet?" Then I try to come up with a solution that meets both our needs as much as possible.

We can usually remove ourselves from situations where others are being emotionally or physically aggressive. When I'm in a situation with a person who is misusing their power or authority, the first thing I do is figure out how I can limit the power they have over me.

This might mean I immediately remove myself physically from their presence. It might mean I have to renegotiate one of my needs so that I'm not dependent upon that person to meet it for me. It might mean I have to change how I feel about the thing I want or need from them and find a way to meet the need for myself. Or it might mean that I firmly state what behavior I will and will not accept from them and ask for a change. *If they refuse to change a behavior that has a substantial negative effect on me I remove myself from them.*

Re-Framing: Imagine the most difficult circumstances of your life turning out a better way.

I used to think that imagining a situation to be different than it really was might be a harmful form of fantasy. Could you disconnect from reality by doing this? Would you lose touch?

In bodywork training designed to release trauma I learned that imagining an **acceptable outcome** to a difficult situation frees the mind and releases the negative energy of that situation. Even a mythical and imagined outcome is healthier than the continuous recycling of trauma. The mind does not care if it is a real or imagined event, it will take directions and act on the visualized scenario if you use enough detail and give it an emotional component or "charge."

There is a Biblical reference to this concept. It says, "For as we think in our hearts so are we...." Proverbs 23:7. This clearly shows us the power of our thoughts.

> **To gain more actual control of your life and environment practice rehearsing possible situations in advance, or reframe past experiences to have a different outcome.**

Specifically, you can take a situation that normally caused you a lot of difficulty or anxiety and imagine yourself feeling calm, confident and in control of yourself and effectively negotiating a positive outcome. For example, I could imagine that when a particular girl from my childhood attacked me, I returned to my memory of the fight and defended myself (instead of what I actually did—which was nothing.) Or I could say, "You must not feel very good about yourself to have to degrade others by spitting on them."

Instead of being passive, I could imagine standing my ground so she'd never dare bother me again. I could visualize that I stood up for myself the first time she scratched, kicked, and spit on me which would have prevented all the times she did this from ever occurring. I could tell my parents that I chose not to associate with people who degraded me and that the situation was not negotiable.

Your whole body might sigh with relief when you visualize a different or more acceptable outcome. The relief is tangible.

> **Application: Take inventory. Analyze which of your characteristics are helping you get what you want out of life.**

Write them down. See if you can find ways to accentuate these more. On your paper list suggestions for capitalizing on your positive traits. Next, honestly evaluate what your self-defeating and negative characteristics are (often survival mechanisms that worked as a youngster to help you cope with trauma but are now hurting you).Write them down on a separate piece of paper. You will be throwing away this sheet of negatives along with a cleansing exercise soon. Its only purpose is to stimulate possible solutions, not to continually dwell on your faults.

Make a firm commitment to change the negative things you have listed. Meditate and pray about possible solutions to change these characteristics. When you can think of a way to offset each of these negative habits or characteristics, write it down on the first sheet of paper along with your other good characteristics and cross out the corresponding negative characteristic on your separate sheet. When you have thought of at least one way to overcome or offset each negative characteristic and you have crossed them all out, it's time for the cleansing process.

Cleansing Process: Set aside a time when you can relax thoroughly. I suggest that you lay down and close your eyes. Take a few deep breaths and visualize yourself acting out each of the positive new ideas created from the old negative list. After you have seen yourself acting out these new ways of behaving and thinking, in your mind, say aloud to yourself: "The old, unproductive ways of thinking are completely over! I am free! In every way I am continuously thinking and behaving in new and productive ways! "

Now get up and tear up the old list saying, "This has nothing to do with me any longer." Then throw it away, burn it, or bury it. Whatever feels the most final and cleansing to you is what you should do with the list. Now let the past be completely done and over. You are becoming the new you. **Welcome to the freedom of being in control of your own thoughts and feelings.**

Faith

I want to share a few very special faith-promoting experiences I have had with my son as a toddler. They helped us both see how much God cares about each of us.

I was taking my son to his swim lessons along with my infant daughter. We were running late and with all of the distractions of belting in two children into car seats and bringing diaper bags, etc, I did not notice that our truck was nearly out of gas. I also forgot to pack a snack for myself to keep my blood sugar stabilized. At that time I would get low blood sugar and get weak, shaky and faint very rapidly at times.

We had the swim lesson and I was feeling like I really needed some food. We were on our way home when the truck ran out of gas in the middle of a very busy five-lane road. My son and I talked about the fact that it wouldn't be very safe for us to walk down the busy road to get gas; we had nothing to put the gas into and I was shaking too much to be able to carry the baby to a gas station.

We decided to have a prayer. My son offered the prayer and asked that we could start the truck and get safely to a gas station. After the prayer, the truck started and we made it safely to a gas station and filled the tank and I got a snack and we went home. We were so thankful for the help. It made a big impression on both of us. **My son has never doubted the power of faith and prayers since that day.**

Another faith promoting experiences occurred when I had filed for divorce and was living alone. I had a very large yard to care for. I had not mowed any lawn more than a couple of times because it wore me out and made me shake (a complication of adrenal insufficiency) and I was allergic to the grass. I had no money to pay someone else to care for it. So one day, since the grass was quite tall, I decided that I needed to mow the lawn.

I tried repeatedly to get the mower to start—unsuccessfully. I was feeling tired and discouraged but I decided to pray. I told my son (then four years old), that I couldn't get the mower to work and I really needed to mow the lawn. I asked if he would join me in prayer. He happily agreed and we asked the Lord to help us get the mower started so we could take care of our lawn. My children's faith always bolsters my own because in their mind when they pray it will always be answered. After the prayer, I expectantly pulled the starter and the mower started immediately. We said a prayer of thanks and my son did a little victory dance in celebration. I thanked the Lord for helping my son and me to remember that He does answer prayers and that He cares about every aspect of our lives.

My illness and other trials gave me an understanding of the enormous power of faith—faith in the Lord to assist me in accomplishing all I want to for good, and faith in myself. I did what was medically impossible—I stayed alive despite repeated health crises that brought me to the brink of death. I knew that my life had been spared several times and I had a strong conviction that there was much more for me to do. I could see the enormous strength, tenacity, and courage I had gained from it. I gained an entirely different perspective of life. I could see that each day we are given precious time. It could be used to enjoy, uplift others and myself, or it could be squandered in pursuit of that which is of minor significance. I never want to lose this perspective of what is real and most important. I now govern my days with this perspective as a guideline. I carefully evaluate the use of my time and fill my hours and days with learning, personal growth and the sheer pleasure and joy that my meaningful relationships bring to me.

My perspective on life is different because I have known the rigors of death firsthand.

I have gained an invaluable insight into the value of life because of my fight against death. *Death is not to be feared unless you have regrets.* If you have something you really want to do for good—a mission in life, it can compel you to fight against all the odds and stay a little longer.

All Things Work Together For Our Good

My religion is Christianity. If this is not yours, you will likely find similar teachings in your religion. Timeless truths are found in many religions and philosophies. *However, they only work if they are completely true.* Please adapt and apply these principles in whatever way feels comfortable to you. I have predominantly used stories from the Bible to illustrate life lessons in the next few chapters.

My belief and faith in God and my understanding of the following principles gave me the courage to persevere in my trials. I believe they will give you inspiration to tackle your challenges.

The "No Room In The Inn" Principle

Consider the physical circumstances of Christ's birth. The simple comforts afforded to the other travel weary people were unavailable, because there was no room for them in the Inn. Joseph and Mary were forced into a stable and there she bore the Son of God.

Such conditions seem abhorrent to us with all our modern conveniences. However, those circumstances were different than our times.

> **"And we know that all things work together for good to them that love God...."Romans 8:28**

Application: This is a strong example of how the Lord can work all things for our good.

The inns in that time period and location were not like a motel today where a clean, private room can be obtained. It was most likely a common room shared by as many people as the innkeeper could crowd in. Imagine these conditions with all of the germs of many strangers, and the noise and bustle that would be present if Mary and Joseph had been able to obtain a place in the Inn. *This would not have been an ideal place for giving birth to a precious newborn.*

With fresh straw, the stable was probably cleaner than the inn and may have had no other human occupants. Mary bore the Son of God in a private place with her husband and likely had angels minister to her as well. In the stable there was room for the humble shepherds, who had been told by the angels to seek this babe, to come and worship their newborn King without the intrusion of bustling onlookers that would likely have been present in a room at the inn. Although it seems like extreme deprivation to us, considering the circumstances of the time, the stable afforded Mary and Joseph the things needed to bring the Christ child into the world.

Learn Timeless True Principles and Live Them

Author's Experience: At first I was banging my head against a brick wall metaphorically, because I was sure that if I just had enough faith and willpower that I would heal and overcome all my difficulties. After many years of pleading and praying to be healed from terrible health problems and to be shielded from victimization in my life, **the answer gently came. I had to learn and live true principles.** The example came to my mind that although Jesus was perfect and sinless, he had to be baptized in order to fulfill God's Law. He could not be saved if He was ignorant to this law or principle.

What I finally realized is that no matter how much faith I exercised or how hard I tried, God could not and would not change the principles that govern the universe just for me. I could not gain relief and peace until I learned and then lived timeless true principles. With this insight that made so much sense, instead of feeling persecuted by God when I was doing everything I knew how to do, I looked for new answers and was led to them.

My prayers were answered—just not in the way I thought they would be. Slowly the things I needed to change about myself were unfolded to me. I realized I had to implement new ways of thinking and relating. I had to quit focusing my prayers on asking that the problems be changed or taken from me and find ways to be actively involved in changing myself! I had to begin problem solving like I never had before. I had to learn to change my actions, which at first created disconcerting changes in my relationships with others. This caused a ripple effect of many changes.

Learn To Change Yourself

When I finally learned I had to change myself—not the circumstances--my whole outlook on life changed.

> **The Lord didn't change the rules for me but gently guided me to an understanding of the truths I needed to heal my life.**

Lesson: *I had always considered myself a peacemaker and played that role at any cost to me.* The cost was too high. I finally felt I had permission to act assertively, which before had seemed wrong. Now I knew I could change myself without feeling condemned.

I began exercising the principles of autonomy, and correct use of thoughts. I learned that my self-worth was not merely about other people's opinion of me. These new thoughts and behaviors came as new ideas and thoughts entered my mind--more answers to prayer. I also remembered how much I loved reading and began to make it a priority to find and read good self-help books. I also had the blessing of a few choice friends and clients who shared their perspective of how their lives worked.

One client wrote down some of her favorite affirmations. I was totally excited about this idea and began making some of my own. I remembered how I had regularly set goals when I was a teenager and I started setting goals again.

Then God gave me the strength to keep working at it until I could apply the affirmations and they became a core part of me. I was guided each step of the way. One of the things I have found so exhilarating is that after I had come to these answers through prayer and meditation, I began finding a few of these principles discussed in some of the self-help books I was reading. *I would get so excited to see that the answers didn't just apply to me, but had universal application.* I also felt humbled to know that the Lord cared enough to personally tutor me and then back up, through others opinions and writings, what I felt I had learned. **Most of these principles have their basis in scripture and I poured over the scriptures to find answers.** It amazed me that something I had read many times before suddenly had new and personal application for my life.

> **Application: I began the practice of just opening the scriptures and reading the passage that fell open.** I cannot count the many times that the exact answer I needed was right before my eyes on the pages.
>
> Make seeking greater insight, spirituality and learning true principles a part of your daily life. We are born with a desire to connect with the infinite and fill the spiritual void that often plagues our lives. This longing can be filled and is an important part in your search to overcome your difficulties. Truth is truth wherever it is found.

The "Job Principle"

Lesson: I have a strong belief in the principle I call the "Job Principle." Of all the stories in the Bible, I can relate most to the life of Job! He was a very righteous man and was always obedient to the Lords commandments. One day Satan told the Lord that He was making it too easy for Job because he had it all—great wealth, a large family, and great spiritual blessings. Satan suggested that the Lord to allow him to take it all away and see if Job would still be so faithful.

He was the wealthiest man in the East and then he lost all his wealth. In one day, he lost all his flocks and herds in various ways and the servants who tended them were also killed. Then Job lost most of his children in a terrible windstorm that collapsed the house they were in. When he heard about all this happening in one day, he... "Rent his mantle, and shaved his head, and fell down upon the ground and worshipped, and said, "Naked came I out of my mother's womb and naked shall I return thither: The Lord gave and the Lord hath taken away; blessed be the name of the Lord."

Next, Satan was allowed to take Job's health by afflicting him with boils from head to foot. Job became repulsive to others because the boils upon his skin contained worms and dust and his breath became very foul. Finally, his friends and wife turned against him. His wife suggested that he curse God and die and his friends came and accused him of committing great evil and bringing the wrath of God upon himself. His friends were falsely accusing him and yet he endured their chastening. **He wished he had never been born at times, but he never gave up his faith nor would he turn away from the Lord.**

Lesson: Because of his great faith and integrity, after the trial of his faith, the Lord compensated him with twice as much of everything that he had before.

In the end all that he had lost was restored and multiplied. He had more children, and many more flocks and herds, his wealth was restored, and his body was restored to perfect health. He praised God!

I believe this to be a real story about a real person who actually lived, if you don't agree, think of it as a powerful metaphor.

The popular myth is that you can affirm and positively think your way through life without any problems if you'd just let go of your negativity. I strongly disagree! **Plainly illustrated is the fact that sometimes we are given trials and adversity to prove us, to strengthen us and to see if we will rise to the challenge with our faith intact. Only after we have met the criteria of the test are we worthy and able to receive the reward or compensation.** Sometimes our trials are a means of influencing and strengthening those close to us who can observe our struggle and have the wisdom to learn from our trials and difficulties.

Sometimes our adversity is self-inflicted and changing our thoughts to positive ones and affirming the good will lift us out of our misery. The great wisdom lies in determining the operating factor in the adversity you are experiencing. If you truly want to know, you will be able to find the answers to your particular problem.

I find it offensive and trite for others to suggest that all of our problems are our own fault. Clearly, the story of Job offers a different perspective. To take this self-righteous judgmental attitude towards others is essentially what Job's friends did, and they were wrong as the Lord proves later in the story. The Lord describes Job as "Perfect and upright"—hardly a description of someone wallowing in self-perpetuated negativity.

Now here is the exciting part, when Job had met the test with faithfulness, he was compensated exponentially.

I believe we can count on this principle as a promise to the faithful—those who are truly seeking to overcome their trials and adversity. You can expect to be compensated. Sometimes it's immediately apparent. *I have strong conviction that this principle has worked in my life.* When I learned true principles about how to govern my actions in the particular situation I was in, and then courageously applied these, I was ready and worthy to be compensated. I have been richly blessed as compensation for all my trials. I have been healed from a terminal illness. I have much more satisfaction in myself and what I have made of my life and I no longer have any tendencies toward being a victim. This is miraculous to me!

I know that however bleak and horrible the circumstances in your life, God can make all things work together for your good. I know this, because it has been proven in my life. You have to keep looking for how He's making it work for you, and what possible benefits you may receive from your afflictions. It will make whatever you have to deal with more bearable and bring you the bright hope that there is a positive purpose in every difficulty and tragedy of our life if we will only allow ourselves to acknowledge it.

I am not suggesting that intentionally breaking the law or violating the principles of truth will eventually work to your benefit. This would be totally incorrect. What I'm saying is that if you have done this and you want a way back, you will be assisted depending on the severity of your violation. Clearly we can only count on this principle to work if we too are like Job in our zeal to do what we understand to be right, and constantly seek for the ultimate truths of the universe.

Whether or not you believe a true principle does not change that it is true! Our actions must be in alignment with true principles, then we have a right to the reward, or blessing that is attached to living it.

Opposition

Opposition is a timeless true principle. We see it everywhere in the world. Everything has its opposite, yin and yang, light and darkness, pleasure and pain, good and evil, etc. We could not grow or experience true joy if we never knew sorrow. We are going to experience some trials and adversity as we progress in this life.

Some have said if you don't have critics you're not growing.

If we diligently seek to find the good or "the lesson in each situation", the Lord is able to provide a reward or blessing for us. If we live the lesson well, we are divinely entitled to reward and compensation.

Along with the principle of opposition comes the principle of deliverance. The Lord always provides a means of deliverance from opposition be that physical, emotional, and sometimes even death! We qualify for that deliverance by living true principles and asking for His help.

It helps when we are humble enough to stick with the opposition until we have learned the lesson and not turn away and blame God.

We are not placed in a situation that we cannot overcome. The means to overcome will be made available. We're not stuck!

These things I have spoken unto you, that in me ye might have peace. In the world ye shall have tribulation: but be of good cheer; I have overcome the world.

John 16:33

Change: Out Of the Fire—The Dynamic Healing Process

After the trial of our faith comes the blessings

> "That the trial of your faith being more precious than of gold that perisheth though it be tried with fire, might be found unto praise and honour and glory at the appearing of Jesus Christ."
>
> 1 Peter 1:7

How do you know what is true?

When my friend Holly asked me if I thought that a certain principle was true, I asked her to turn the principle around and ask herself, "What would happen if it wasn't true?"

What results have living this principle given you in your life? Have you benefited from it?

- Does it make your quality of life and thoughts better? She answered that her life had improved from living the principle.

- I suggested that maybe it was worthwhile to live the principle if it brought good things to her life. This is one of the tests to determine if something is a good and true principle. If it works and brings you closer to your highest spiritual values, and living it brings good things—it's probably a true principle.

> I used to think that God must not love me to let so many bad things happen to me, but then I had several beautiful spiritual experiences that enveloped me in God's love and I knew that my perspective was confused.

I came to an understanding that God loved me very much and did not want me to experience so much pain, but He does not override the agency of others. He was waiting to show me the true, unchanging, principles that would change my life and lead me out of the pain a step at a time. The idea came to me that He would not change the principles that governed the universe just because I had a strong desire and faith that the situation could be different. I had to seek out the true principles and live them in order for my life to change.

Author's Experience: I used to think that my painful experiences in life were like an onion. As I peeled open the layers of pain and terror a layer at a time, I was afraid there would be nothing left when I was finished. I felt afraid that I could not fully examine the depths of pain that were locked into my body and brain or I would simply die from the process. I cannot express adequately in words the exquisite emotional pain and terror that I felt from some of the experience I've been subjected to.

Jenny explains a similar feeling like this: It was as if each time I began to remember my experiences of betrayal, abuse, emotional and physical pain, my mind would shut down, like a steel door shutting forcibly! I could not actually hold onto the thoughts in my mind for very long before I just shut down and forgot what I was thinking about, or dissociated from the pain as if it had happened to someone else. This happened repeatedly when I went for counseling. I would either feel like I was re-living the horror with all the physical symptoms including being cold, shaking, feeling nauseated, and anxious, or I could dissociate or tell it like it was a story and I was completely emotionally detached.

I often felt like I just wanted to scream and run away from whatever had just triggered a painful memory. This went on for years until I was unwilling to re-experience the pain. It seemed locked in my body and no amount of talking about it changed the feelings inside!

Author's Lesson: Instead of thinking of myself as an onion, I now hold the image of a prized rosebush when I think of my painful experiences. The only way to get a rose to grow to its full potential is to prune it. Cut away the dead wood and many of the unproductive branches. The old painful experiences had to be cut away, and while it was painful at times as I acknowledged the experiences, by "cutting them away". Then new vigorous growth appeared and crowning it all was a glorious rose of exquisite beauty and fragrance—it is me! Of course along with every rose there are the thorns which represent my protective barriers that I have finally established that keep me safe and also the painful experiences that helped shape me into the rose I have become.

> **Application: When you begin to see yourself as valuable and worthwhile, the world will begin to reflect that back to you.**

One of the most helpful things I affirm to myself is: "I am not invested in other people's opinion of me." It is really hard to actually do this. I have found that it is the most negative and abusive people who are intent on breaking down my self-esteem so that they can more easily manipulate me. When you live true to your own value system (if it's based on truth and goodness) you can more easily brush off criticism and maintain self-esteem.

When you formulate an action plan to overcome your weaknesses you will receive opposition from others who want to keep things in status quo but you will also receive unexpected strength and fortitude to overcome. When you cultivate an unwavering desire to make positive changes in your life, the universe will rally to bring those things to you. Try it and see!

Change Begins With Problem Solving

Changing Our Emotions To Suit Our Needs

Some people feel that there are positive and negative emotions. In most cases, I think that emotions are neutral but the behaviors we act out as an expression of them can be detrimental or positive. For instance, anger can be a powerful force for action to protect yourself, or make a needed change, or it can grow to rage and murder. The choice is in the behavior. If you rage often the expression of anger may not be the healthiest way to heal. You may need to practice abstaining from the expression of anger. For instance, you could say to yourself when you are feeling rage start to rise, "I am calm and under control. I can handle this without hurting anyone with my fists or my words." You get the picture.

See my Anger Affirmations in the **Appendix F,** for an expression of healthy ways to look at anger and help to transform it into positive change.

When you change your thoughts you can change your behavior and feelings, and you can master self-control. This is the most critical element in overcoming adversity.

> **We have the power to change our emotions if we change our thoughts. We can actually substitute an emotion we don't want to feel anymore with another more suitable one.**

I Am a Survivor!

I am a survivor of surreal trauma and violence that was relentless and ongoing. I spent part of every day from the time I have conscious memory figuring out how to stay out of danger, and recover from the aftermath of the choices of my perpetrators.

I had to reach deep inside of me and empower the parts of me **screaming for safety, love, and a shot at happiness.** If I had not exercised this kind of mental toughness and learned to release the suffering and trauma--I would have died!

If I had not learned how to channel the inner strength inside me, I would have died from Secondary Adrenal Insufficiency, from someone trying to kill me, or I might have just given up.

Having my life threatened-- multiple times, was just the tip of the iceberg! I know what it's like to feel helpless and hopeless, and that is a special kind of suffering that is far too familiar to other survivors and I want to help you end that kind of suffering. I want to help you to choose to LIVE, and experience joy, passion and health.

Instead of living in misery, I developed unshakeable determination to limit the power of the abusive people in my life-- and not just survive but to **turn my trials into triumphs!**

My mental toughness was born of pain, injury, suffering, and a determination to heal.

This book is not just a history of my stories of suffering-- but a guide to TRIUMPH that shows you how to overcome whatever difficulty you face in your own life!

"Happiness depends more on the inward disposition of mind than on outward circumstances."--Benjamin Franklin

Abuse

My History of Being Abused:

Here's a little about my history. I include it not because I want to blame others, just to illustrate that we can continue in our misery; feeling helpless, hopeless and feeling like we have no personal power OR we can become a Phoenix and recreate ourselves and our lives into what we want!

What makes me think that I'm qualified to write a book on overcoming adversity, and trauma, is illustrated in the next few paragraphs. My emphasis in this book is on victory and overcoming rather than continuously dwelling on the trauma. I believe you can overcome whatever you need to heal from, to live a life of joy and fulfillment with the resources in my book.

My home of origin: There was a pattern of emotional and physical abuse in my home of origin. I suffered severe physical abuse from being beaten repeatedly by my mother at the ages of five and younger until objects like brooms, yardsticks, and wooden spoons were broken over my buttocks and kidneys. I was then sent to my room and not allowed to leave, often not even to use the toilet.

Emotional abuse was very prevalent in my home. I was repeatedly threatened with bodily harm or death in my home with comments from my mother like, "Your father is so strong his fists should be registered as lethal weapons. He could kill someone with his bare hands-- don't make him mad!" I had an enormous fear of my father. I had seen him become so angry that I did fear for my safety, and I had been beaten severely by him as well.

When my sister and I were molested by a neighbor babysitting us (when I was the age of three) and the perpetrator told me not to tell ANYONE because if I did my dad would be so mad that he might kill me, I believed it and wouldn't talk about it.

When I was four years old, a relative was invited to live in our home. My parents knew that he had been previously arrested for exhibitionism. He masturbated regularly in front of my sister and me.

I was never allowed to express anger or sorrow, with threats like, "shut up or I'll give you something to cry about". No one could express an opinion that was contrary to my parents without extreme sanctions.

As a teenager, I was grounded once for an entire summer because I didn't make my bed everyday. My parents took away Christmas (all the presents) because I woke up and talked to our neighbors on walkie-talkies on Christmas Eve. Then when relatives came for dinner they humiliated us by saying that Santa didn't come for us because I woke up and scared him away.

Unfortunately, because of my background and inadequate skills in personal relationships and self-defense, I was continuously involved in deeply destructive relationships.

By the time I was in college, a professor got me down on the floor during private vocal instruction and under the guise of teaching how to use my diaphragm to breathe properly, straddled me pushing his crotch against my pelvis before I could stop the situation. On another occasion, he stroked my breast while again talking about "proper breathing". He was always telling me how attractive my body was and interrogated me about who I'd been with and whether I held their hand or kissed them. I told my mother about it and she told me not to report it because he was in charge of my vocal scholarship and she didn't want to pay for it. I left the University to get away from him and my trust in humanity was waning considerably.

From my childhood on my relationships seemed to always be a source of pain and fear. I seemed to endlessly attract people who treated me with contempt, domination, and abuse. Intimate relationships were a disastrous experience. Some of the things I lived through seem so incredible and horrifying that sometimes it's hard to even think about them. It's also hard for many people to hear about them.

Not surprisingly, I chose abusive partners even though I tried hard not to. My partner was an expert in mental abuse. He constantly kept me in a state of turmoil. He would scream at me when I brought the groceries home because he didn't like something I bought or made for us to eat. I was often punished for the same meal that was something he had said he liked and ate the week before at our home. If I cooked a meal that we had eaten at his parents' house, he would say I was feeding him "garbage" and storm out of the house saying he was not coming back. Eventually, he did come back but I never knew if he was going to or not.

He found a song that I strongly disliked so he bought a copy of it and would play it over and over again singing along with it at the top of his voice. He would physically prevent me from turning it off.

He would cuddle up to me in bed and kick me in the legs or back and when I pulled away and told him to stop, **he would say he had not done anything and I was just imagining it!** He once left me in sub-zero weather at a theater at 1:00 am with no way to get home since he took the car, because I stopped to talk to a friend briefly on the way out after the movie.

When I was in excruciating abdominal pain because of a kidney stone traveling through my urinary tract, he insisted on having sex! When I refused, he became infuriated. I was dehydrated, too weak to walk on my own, and was vomiting profusely because the stone still had not passed. He refused to bring me a drink of water to help me get some liquid to re-hydrate. **Then he left—taking the only telephone with him so I could not call anyone else for help.** (This was long before cell phones and Uber). Amazingly someone showed up at my door and took me to the hospital where I was admitted for surgery and kept there for several days. He didn't come to the hospital to check on me for days.

Another time, he taunted me with my pet turtle who had died by putting it in a bag and shoving it in my face repeatedly, while literally dancing around the room mocking me while I cried.

After an argument, he pretended to make up to me by asking me to come over to him so he could hug me. I went to him and he said he was sorry, and held my face in his hands, then he began laughing hysterically and he wouldn't tell me why. I went to look in a mirror and discovered that he had wiped a huge, green booger, on my cheek to humiliate me.

He became fixated on thoughts of death and violence. He bought a combat knife and told me how the blood groove worked when you wanted to stab someone repeatedly. Without it, he explained to me, you couldn't pull the knife out because of the suction created in the tissue around the knife. He began carrying the knife with him everywhere for "just in case." Soon he began to talk about death all the time which finally lead him to threatening to murder me, cut me into pieces and dump my body in a garbage dumpster. He went so far as to provide me with the sound effects of how my body parts would sound as they hit the bottom of the dumpster!

He got quite violent with me a number of times and when I tried to run away from him he would chase me and scratch me or tackle me and pull me back inside the apartment. He told me I would never get away from him even if I tried, and that if I did he'd hunt me down or kill me or one of my siblings who was 18 months old. Eventually the abuse escalated until he nearly murdered me.

I was saved by a very strong warning—in the form of a premonition—that told me I was going to be killed. I was then told exactly what to say and do in order to avoid it. I thank God, for helping me and saving my life with a warning.

I was able to obtain a *permanent restraining order* against him. I count myself lucky to be alive! It was years before I could actually talk about the details of what happened when he tried to kill me. After that he stalked me through 3 states for several years.

My parents were not what I consider emotionally supportive of me after I ended that relationship, *although they said they wanted to help*. Throughout the relationship, they continuously reminded me of what poor choices I had made in choosing my partner. They said I should have known better. They acted as though I should have to suffer because of my poor choices in a partner. They had the attitude of "You made your bed now sleep in it." They continuously told me they didn't want to hear about any problems I had in my relationship. I was an adult and was supposed to handle it by myself.

My mother physically attacked me as late as the age of twenty-one. My family came to visit me at my apartment so they could meet my fiancé, that I met after leaving the monster! Mother was angry with my fiancé for something *he did,* but instead of taking it up with him she waited until he boarded a plane and was in another state. Then, in my own apartment with my siblings present, she started verbally attacking me, saying that my fiancé shouldn't have told my siblings *to clean up after themselves.* I said I wasn't even around when he said it and it didn't have anything to do with me, and she should talk to him.

This so enraged her that she threw me against a wall which slammed my head into the wall and then began beating my hands with a hairbrush. (It broke my pinky finger and it was sore for many days.) I was very angry but I just looked at her, then she started screaming for my father to come in and **hold me down so she could beat me more effectively.**

The irony is that I didn't even try to defend myself, yet she kept telling me I had better get control of myself **because she didn't like the way I was looking at her!**

When my father came in, he took one look at me and decided not to hold me down. I left my family in my apartment and went for a long drive.

For years, she told anyone who would listen to her that I was an **"animal with a bad temper" and that "I was completely out of control—because I had dared to look at her with anger in my eyes!"**

My reality is that if I wasn't in complete control of myself I would have defended myself and beaten her senseless, especially since I had just been through a horrifying experience with my partner who had threatened to kill me and nearly succeeded. My fight or flight reflexes were on red alert!

Another partnership proved horribly damaging. There were years of emotional abuse. On our first vacation, he explained he might have to leave me because I had not folded his clothes properly when I placed them in his suitcase. If I didn't place the food properly in the cupboard I was severely chastised. (It was literally alphabetized.)

I have an exaggerated startle response because of repeated threats against my life, and physical and emotional abuse my whole life. So he hid in dark rooms and grabbed my ankles to frighten me as I walked by. He did this when I was pregnant and had already miscarried 6 children.

This was terrifying to me and very amusing to him. He refused to allow me to make my own decisions about how to spend my time, my money and many other issues. His drive in life was to create conflict. He would instigate a problem and try to provoke me into a fight- constantly. There was so much more but this gives an overview of the trauma.

Eventually my physical health failed! I developed a terminal illness that was a direct result of the extraordinary stress to my system—**a lifetime of fight or flight can be fatal!** I realized I had to leave this man to survive.

With life threatening health problems, two children to care for, and extraordinary stress trying to deal with the break-up of my relationship; my parents "moved in for the kill". They tried to force me to let them "take care of me." Their idea of caring for me was to take all my possessions, including about $40,000 worth of equity in my home, my privacy, and all of my personal freedoms. I remembered all too clearly how they treated me when I lived in their home as a child. I told them NO! I faced them down and told them they shouldn't even try forcing me to do what they wanted.

I knew they would not be able to force their agenda. I was strong enough to stand up to them and I had a good attorney who was very supportive of me. I talked to him about the stuff they were trying to do. He was absolutely astounded and disgusted!

Later in a phone conversation, my parents started in on me again with their agenda. I told them again, I would not let them move in and take over my life. At this point, my father was so enraged that he began yelling and swearing at me. When I said, "You can't swear at me, or assault me anymore, I have had a lifetime of abuse," he became belligerent and said he would never speak to me again. **He didn't for many years and neither did my mother. I had an unexplained urge to call him on Father's Day when we had our last conversation. He was killed suddenly in an auto accident 4 days later!**

It was very painful to be disowned and I grieved terribly for months. I got a lot of messages from others (church) that I was a bad person for not "honoring" my parents. **I held my ground and in the end it was the best thing that could have happened. I began to heal and become the person I wanted and needed to be. I learned the lessons I share in this book.**

My injuries from perpetrators have required several reconstructive surgeries to counter the effects of physical abuse.

These experiences are just the tip of the iceberg, but I think sufficient evidence to help the reader understand I've experienced some suffering and grief and I have had a few issues to work through.

I feel I'm a qualified opinion on trauma, abuse, adversity, and how to move past it.

Overcoming Abuse:

If you grow up in an abusive environment, you are not destined to be victims forever or to automatically become abusers, otherwise God would not be just. Why would he set us up for something we could not possibly avoid? There is way out! You can, and must change your behavior whether your life has followed a pattern of victimization or you have been an abuser.

Jenny expressed the pain of abuse like this: "I have experienced many forms of abuse, but the most devastating form to me was the mental and emotional abuse that attacks your mind and your spirit in ways that are so hard to overcome. Long after the physical blows heal, the words remain to hold you down, hold you back and make you believe the abuse is all *your* fault. The power plays and programming (telling you how to think and what to do) is far more insidious than the physical trauma of abuse.

I learned that to break free of the abuse, the changes had to occur with my behavior. I formulated a plan to break free. I started thinking about what I wanted my life to be like, not what it was. I spent many hours in contemplation, about why I was willing to be abused just because I wanted to be a "peacemaker" and turn the other cheek. I thought that to be a good Christian I had to continue to forgive and never protest what I felt inside was so wrong. I had internalized "The Beatitudes" to the point that I couldn't see things clearly. I couldn't see past my fears. I was afraid that if I protested or left an abusive relationship, I would have failed somehow and God would be displeased. Gradually, I reasoned that I wasn't much use dead, and that I had come too far to die from the next attack. I realized that it was not my purpose to live or die this way. I had to change!"

Lesson: Too often we believe what others tell us we are such as, "worthless, weak, incapable, etc." We believe it when they say, "You deserve this."

> **Application: When you are ready to change, the resources you need will manifest themselves and people and ideas combine miraculously to assist you.**

Author's Experience: Because of the threats of assault I repeatedly received, I decided I wanted to feel safer. I found and read some incredibly helpful books about how to get out of my pattern of unhealthy passiveness. By thinking differently and then acting differently, I learned to recognize the signs that things were escalating to violence or violation of my boundaries in my work and everywhere else.

I rehearsed physically and mentally a plan of action instead of freezing up in fear or trying to minimize the situation in my mind until I was really in danger. I took a self-defense training class that was very empowering. There I learned a power posture and how to use my voice firmly and to say things like "Don't come any closer, or I'll consider it an attack!" I learned to fight full force in a very supportive environment. I felt what it was like to fight through realistic assault situations. I knew I could deliver a knockout blow in a matter of seconds. I learned to trust my intuition and "inner knowing" of potentially dangerous people or situations. I have continued my martial arts training for many years now. Next, I developed a game plan to change how I felt when I was being threatened with unwanted touching or physical assault. I learned to speak out and set clear boundaries with consequences attached. I learned to say, "This is not going to work anymore, I won't allow you to treat me this way or talk to me this way." I began to feel and believe that I could stop the abuse, by my words, actions, or leaving if necessary. I began to feel a sense of worth that I had not known before. I knew my course of action was right for me and that the changes I made would benefit me, and my children. I could teach my children and others how to be assertive and set appropriate verbal and physical boundaries. I want my children to experience a life free from abuse.

Expect opposition to you changing! As I learned new ways of relating and made rapid changes in my personality, I was continually challenged. The people who had been violating my boundaries did not want me to change the status quo. New people entered my life that also challenged me but I would not be pushed back into the ineffective ways of relating.

Somatic Memories and Trauma

As a massage therapist, I was introduced to the concept of "Somatic Memory". I learned that experiences that happen when we are severely stressed or traumatized remain locked in our bodies and minds. They remain there waiting for further resolution exactly intact as you first experienced them. I learned and began to use bodywork techniques to unlock the cellular memories of trauma from my body and to assist others in doing so. This was life-altering healing!

> **Application: We can use positive thinking to get out of a situation, but if it persists despite all our goals, affirmations, and positive thinking, re-evaluate the situation.**
>
> Ask yourself, "Is there another purpose for what I'm experiencing? Have I set the right goals? Are my objectives honorable and do my actions benefit others?"

Some of our experiences are for the benefit and learning of others, not just the result of our negative thoughts. Sometimes we remain in a situation until we have learned the lesson of that situation. Sometimes we are a link to others—their lives are changed because you shared the process of your learning with them. Not every situation is under our control.

Sometimes we are a prop in someone else's play. The principle of personal agency and accountability affords each person the ability to make bad and sometimes evil choices. Sometimes those choices have devastating consequences to you, through no fault of your own.

Sometimes we are the only person who could help another through a problem of their own because of invaluable experience gained in overcoming a trial of our own.

Teach Others to Solve Their Own Problems

Share with them your wisdom *if they ask for it*. Most people won't take unsolicited advice. Begin by teaching them at the level they are at emotionally. If they have been in a situation where most decisions were made for them and enforced, how will they understand how to make wise choices of their own? This can be the case in adults who have been involved with overbearing or abusive people and through their submissiveness never learned their own capabilities and personal power. Empower them to learn and grow beyond their starting point.

> **God works through people to help his children. Listen and watch for opportunities to uplift your fellowman. When we serve, we bless not only those we serve, but our own lives as well.**

My friend Holly had very childlike perceptions of her own choices and personal power. Helping her to see beyond her old limitations was the beginning of a new life for her— one with adult choices.

We love those that we offer compassionate service to. Usually they love us in return and we bond for the benefit of both parties. Jesus was the greatest example of service.

Sometimes people form bonds because of trauma and form unhealthy bonds with their abusers or perpetrators. This is often seen with abuse survivors.

Learn To Let Go Of Fear!

Author's Experience: One day I determined to step out of the cycle of fear that engulfed my life. As a young woman, I was inappropriately pursued relentlessly by many acquaintances, strangers and authority figures in my life that made unwanted sexual advances. One disturbing experience that I recall involved an authority figure that was in charge of whether I passed my state licensure to sell hearing aids. I naively trusted him and he locked me in his place of business, when I thought we were conducting a legitimate business transaction, and forced a kiss on me instead. I wanted nothing like this from the individual. I was extremely upset because I didn't see it coming. Another individual chased me around the office where I worked and forced me onto the desk then laid on top of me. My boss thought it was pretty amusing. I had to fight him off. Things got much more serious than this in several other instances.

I had been victimized repeatedly as a child. I had been forced to interact and "trust" people who hurt me from my earliest days. As I grew up I learned to dissociate from my feelings of distrust and fear just to survive. I had learned to tune out a lot of inappropriate sexual gestures and comments just to function. But I found that some people were so aggressive I had to fight them off because I essentially ignored their advances until it was too late. I felt like I couldn't win either way.

I had several experiences when I was spared from threatened impending assault. I reasoned with myself that if I had been spared several times already I could reasonably count on being spared in the future as well.

So, why was I so afraid? I was protesting being so close to impending assault or death that I was looking my attacker in the eye and feeling the terror that it evokes. I would do almost anything to avoid it. **Yet, all my fear seemed to energize and attract abusive people.** I eventually learned to set some verbal boundaries and physical boundaries and quit minimizing inappropriate behavior. Now things don't escalate like they did before. Instead of being passive for the sake of keeping the peace, I had to learn to be assertive.

> **Fear energizes the power of adversity and attracts negative experiences to us.**

Lesson: I decided to exercise all the faith I could muster and believe that I would be continually protected until it was time for me to leave this earth. I decided to trust that I had learned new ways of relating that would help shield me from predators. I chose to believe that past was over and I could be safe in the present. I prayed to have a feeling of peace and safety and for continued protection. Then every time I felt fear creeping in I stopped immediately to examine why I was feeling fear. Was there really any danger present or was I slipping back into old habits of thought? I imagined myself being constantly escorted and protected by unseen heavenly beings or "guardian angels" as some people call them. I did this for several months, whenever fear had been triggered for me. I thought of heavenly protection and I felt a rush of peace each time. **I actually believe that any time I need assistance beyond my own strength I can call on God for that heavenly assistance to protect me as long as I am living my life doing good.**

A huge turning point came when I went to talk with a trusted friend (Fredric) about my feelings of never being safe. I explained in overview some of my hideous assault experiences and he looked me straight in the eye and said, **"You are Safe!"** He repeated it several times in different ways and he had such a resolute calmness about it that I believed it! It was very helpful at the time to hear his assessment of how others perceived me. He helped me realize that I was safe and that I no longer projected "deer in the headlights" victim energy. This was very helpful in my confidence level.

> **Application: I believe that heavenly assistance and added strength can be available to each of us if we seek it.**

However, I don't think wearing a little angle pin is going to provide you with protection. Acknowledge that the real source of protection comes from God. If you decide to wear an angel pin understand it is only a reminder of the protective power available to us through a loving God. There is no power in a pin made in the likeness of an angel.

What is it we have to fear? Death, loneliness, loss of relationships and possessions and loss of health are some possibilities. When you begin to trust yourself to overcome all obstacles and trials the power of fear is greatly diminished. It has no power over you to overcome you. While you are feeling uplifted by faith you forget about your fears. Exercise faith in your own abilities to succeed. Exercise faith in God to assist you in your desires to overcome your trials.

Exercise: Take a few minutes to identify some of your core fears. List them here.

____

____

____

____

____

____

When fears or worries are written down they are now "Out of your body" or at least beginning to be. What steps could you take to diminish your worst fears?

____

____

____

____

Take the next week and specifically work with only one core fear. Take some of the steps listed above and record how your fear has dissipated or left.

See the Majesty of Yourself

Lesson: A lot of people have ideas about self-esteem. It is the core of a healthy person. But how do you get self-esteem if you don't have it already?

It starts with a basic understanding of who we are. I believe that each of us has inherent worth because we are living human beings. Our ability to think, reason, and adapt to various situations sets us apart from the animal kingdom. Although animals share some of these characteristics, our skills and talents are far superior in many ways. We have a stewardship to care for the planet and the animals but I don't think they are our peers or our ancestors, or that their rights and abilities exceed ours as humans. We have basic nobility because we are human.

Beyond that, I believe we were created by a loving Divine Creator, and that we are endowed with specific gifts and talents unique to each individual.

> **The circumstances of when and where you were born and the place where you are now in your relationships, work environment, and educational background are all tools you are given to build your life into what you will make of yourself.**

No one else can do exactly what you can do or be exactly who you can be if you will develop your talents, skills, and leadership. This may all sound a bit cliché but if we really examine it in depth it should elevate our basic concept of ourselves as being incredibly valuable. I feel we were meant to be here at this time in history, and in the specific circumstances where we find ourselves. You have the perfect launching pad for your highest potential right now.

It doesn't matter where you have been, as much as it matters where you are going!

- When you take the initiative to begin searching for your talents, skills and attributes that are positive and helpful, you can begin to appreciate yourself more fully. Quit dwelling on all the negative qualities you have! You probably think about them constantly and rehearse them in your mind telling yourself what a rotten person you really are. How helpful can that be? This is one of the factors that keep us from feeling esteem for ourselves. We talk to ourselves in our minds and possibly out loud about all the mistakes we make, what poor judgment we have, and all the rotten things that happen to us etc.

- Have you ever noticed how we often dismiss compliments when we receive them? We frequently question the motivation of the person giving the compliment, or we argue with them about it like, "Oh you like this outfit? I found it at the back of the closet, I don't really like it but I haven't done the laundry this week so I wore it." It leaves the other person wondering if you question their taste in complimenting you and makes it unlikely they will want to do it again.

- **We often internalize as true most of the negative labels that people place on us.** This is a recipe for disaster. You will continually have negative feelings about yourself as long as you accept negative labels about yourself as true.

- **When someone criticizes you, before you take it in and feel bad about yourself, think:** "What might his or her motivation be in saying this?" (This is an appropriate time to question motivation). Most importantly, ask yourself "Is this true about me?" If there is some truth in it, then say to yourself, "I recognize this as an area I'd like to improve in", and write down an action plan to change that characteristic or behavior about yourself. Make an affirmation statement to back it up and cement it in your subconscious mind. For instance, if you are habitually late for work and your boss says, "You're never on time, shape up or you'll lose your job!" If it's true, then change it. If the reason for your lateness is because you never know where you put your keys, then say to yourself, "I always know where I put my keys." I enjoy the benefits of always arriving a few minutes early to work."

- **What you continue to say to yourself, or allow others to say to you, will become true for you**. We will always have detractors in our lives. We must learn to get over their negativity. If it's simply not true about you, forget about it, or challenge them on it. Ask them "Why would you say such a thing about me?" Or make the statement, "You must feel pretty lousy about yourself to have to say such negative things about someone else."

Here's an exercise designed to get your mind thinking of all the great things about you. Let's face it, if you can't figure it out, it will be a lot harder for others to recognize your worth and reflect it back to you.

On the following graph list your qualities under: "My qualities, talents, and blessings." Now take the time to write down all the things you view as your strengths and quality characteristics, talents and blessings you have in your life. Take as many sheets as you need to do this. This is very important because you will be referring to it later when you feel discouraged. Your list may include things like, "I have a great smile, a playful laugh, a good sense of humor. I understand other people's feelings. I have a great desire to learn and change. I am a contribution to the company I work for or the people in my life. I develop new skills on a regular basis. I have many friends.

On the other side of the paper label it "What I am working to develop and receive." Then list the qualities, blessings, and talents you want to have or develop. If you have a supportive person in your life, this exercise could be done together with each of you contributing to the other's list of "My qualities, talents and blessings." It can be a richly rewarding experience for both of you and something you will treasure forever. **Keep the list!**

Exercise:

My Qualities, Talents and Blessings:	What I'm Working to Develop/Receive:

Lesson: One thing I found helpful was trying to imagine my ideal self, or my highest spiritual self. I wondered about how I looked beyond the packaging of the body I now walk around in. Who am I really inside? As I searched myself for the answers, I tapped into the majesty of my soul, and became intimately acquainted with my highest spiritual self.

Here is how I pictured my inner self. I am fearless and wear a sword at my side. It symbolizes my fight against injustice, tyranny and abuse. I never shy away from battle or confrontation because I am fighting for the noblest cause-**personal freedom**. The sword reminds me to "keep up the good fight," and serves as a visible warning to others that I can protect myself from the attacks of others. I am never the aggressor but I'm incredibly strong and able to defend myself when needed. I am standing on a mountain and from this vantage point I can see out over large expanses, giving me perspective and wisdom. I can see things coming at me before they can get to me so I am prepared and ready. The wind whips through my long, full hair and a storm is rolling in with dark clouds—but I am not afraid! I am shielded by protective armor that is symbolic to me and protects me from difficulties of any nature. I feel incredibly majestic, regal, peaceful, and gracious. I am healthy and trim. I cannot be conquered. **I am Indomitable!**

Gradually, I began to see my outer self as I imagined my inner self. The change in my feelings about myself was so profound that several people who had known me for years expressed that my countenance had changed and I looked more peaceful and happier.

A few times in my life when I felt completely overwhelmed, I watched the movie Braveheart over and over. It moved me on a cellular level, both because I have Scottish ancestry, and because I could relate to the character of William Wallace and his struggle, betrayal, and fight to the end for a greater cause. I also despise tyranny and abuse of power in any form. The cry on my lips and in my heart is also **"FREEDOM!"**

Symbolism:

In contemplating my life and its challenges I realized that symbolism is very significant and healing for me.

I have learned that our subconscious mind works predominately with pictures, metaphors and symbols. So I have objects that trigger me to remember my highest cause. I bought a Celtic sword pin that I wear on my coat and at times on other apparel. People are intrigued by it and ask me about it. I tell them it reminds me to "keep up the good fight." Beyond that, it reminds me of the price I have paid for freedom and the price others have paid to give me many of the freedoms I enjoy. It reminds me of the freedoms I enjoy—freedom of thought, freedom of speech, freedom of religion, and many others. It also reminds me to be a key player in the fight of good against evil. I bought an ink stamp with a rampant lion (side-facing and standing) and the word "Freedom" on it. It inspires me. I keep it where I can see it frequently.

To me freedom encompasses the freedom that comes from being able to control your own thoughts and attitudes, and to look outside the parameters and double binds we can be faced with. This is the deepest level of freedom to me. Even though others could take control over our outer environment and we might possibly be coerced into doing things we don't want to do or don't agree with by individuals, groups, governments, employers, we always have the freedom to choose how we will think and react in a given situation. It's about taking responsibility for our thoughts and actions and changing our behaviors and environment when possible. **This is the essence of my message.**

Application: Get to know your ideal self and become that person.

Creative imagery or visualization can be a key to unlocking your inner majesty. Symbols are the language of the subconscious mind and if carefully planned can be very helpful in overcoming your weaknesses. It's important to pick the right symbol.

I wear a ring that is an Alexandrite stone. It changes color in different light settings from pinkish purple to bluish purple and sometimes looks teal. It's a large stone and highly visible and I consider it quite beautiful. It reminds me of myself. I am highly adaptable, ever-changing and radiate beauty from within.

Let's Talk About Our Outer Image

I strongly feel our society places far too much emphasis on the outer packaging. One of the most important things we can learn in life is to accept our bodies and love them for the work of art they really are. No matter what your body looks like, it has kept you alive, and for that it deserves to be honored and cared for. I know that a distorted body image causes some individuals to do such self destructive things that they die trying to look like the picture perfect models we see in the media. I think this is a tragedy! I have struggled with this concept myself. I used to have a gorgeous body that attracted a lot of attention. It was a huge component of my self-esteem and what I thought about myself. I didn't really have the need to reach far beyond the packaging. I developed my intellect and personality also but I loved feeling beautiful.

Fat as Protection: **After I had several experiences where I was threatened with rape, I began to form a protective layer (called fat) around me to ward off some of the attention!**

It created a false sense of security but the inappropriate advances stopped. Yet each time I looked in the mirror I hated the image of my body. I didn't even recognize myself. As I continued in my life and was challenged with terrible health problems and had to take steroid medication to treat my health problems, the option of becoming thin again was very limited. Now my self-image was really threatened. Who was I if I wasn't thin and desirable? I really didn't know for a while. It was quite unsettling. **I had to go really deep within myself and challenge my acceptance of our societal values for thin bodies.**

Lesson: When I became clear about all of the other valuable qualities and characteristics I have, I emerged with an understanding of my inner beauty that far surpassed the outer beauty I once enjoyed. As I fully accepted myself for who I really am, I grew to honor and respect my body for the miracle of still being alive despite all the times I have been extremely ill. I'm alive! It' a miracle! Whenever I start to lament about the loss of my youthful body, I stop and affirm the glory of the strong, resilient, persevering body that I am blessed with. I have less concern over the packaging and I feel like a much more balanced person.

Love the body you have been given. It's exactly the way it needs to be for you to get you what you need out of life. I also believe that we should care for our bodies the best we can so they can care for us a long time.

How people respond to what we project:

Lesson:. I tried an interesting experiment one time. I went to the grocery store and I decided to see if it was the feelings I was projecting about myself that was determining how people reacted to me, or the actual image of my overweight body that they saw. **I tried projecting the confidence I used to have about having a beautiful face and body. I began to walk the way I used to walk when I was competing in beauty pageants and held my head up and project mentally "I'm beautiful." The most amazing thing happened! I had 6 men stop to talk to me and comment on what I was wearing or just**

try to strike up a conversation! Three of them were pretty cute and younger than I was. It didn't matter that I was 60 pounds overweight. **It was all about what I was projecting.** I was stunned! I really learned something by that.

Application: The thoughts we think are what we embody and they are broadcast very clearly to people who choose to tune in to them.

If you believe you're beautiful despite your imperfections, people will respond to you as though you are beautiful. The reciprocal is also true, and applies to all areas of your life. If you think you're ugly, stupid, unworthy of wealth or attention that is what you'll broadcast, and likely what you will receive.

Whatever you think about yourself will be projected loud and clear. Be clear about what you're projecting!

Acknowledge and affirm the inner beauty of other individuals. Challenge your acceptance of the "ideal body" that is pushed on us by the media. Take good care of the body you have been given. It kept you alive, and for that it deserves to be honored and cared for.

Humor Heals

If you want to be happy act like it! Remind your face to look happy. Smile at almost everyone you see. It's rewarding to see the shock in some people's face because a stranger actually smiled at them. Learn to laugh easily and freely-- you may live longer.

I learned to laugh despite my circumstances and when I couldn't believe that anything could get worse, it did. So I laughed because I felt that if I cried I might never be able to stop.

> **Humor goes a long way toward healing and forgiving. The sooner you can laugh after a crisis the sooner you can heal and let go of the trauma.**

Experience: I have always had the ability to laugh off stress and trauma. Once when I was in the emergency room for heart problems, the doctor commented that although I was presenting heart attack symptoms, he didn't think I was having a heart attack because I was laughing. I told him it was my way of coping with severe stress when I felt I couldn't change the situation. **He had no idea of how traumatic my life really was at that time.**

Through laughter, trauma can be resolved immediately instead of getting stored in the mind/body for further resolution. I have found laughter to be great medicine in my life! "Laugh it off!"

I also have a quick wit and see humor in a lot of situations that would not make other people laugh. People often comment on how they enjoy being around me because I frequently laugh and can see the humor in most any crisis. I've read that laughter produces chemicals called endorphins within our bodies that help to counteract the effects of stress and in some cases even affecting disease. **I believe that learning to laugh frequently and finding the lighter side of every situation will go a long way toward helping you cope with whatever difficulty you encounter.**

Lesson: Learn to laugh about a situation instead of laughing at a person. I have seen sarcasm be a very destructive force in a relationship. Sarcasm often couches a very cutting insult in the framework of laughter and leaves the person the sarcasm is directed at wondering "Do they really mean that or think that about me?" I feel strongly that teasing is only funny if both people are enjoying it, otherwise it can cross over to destructive and even abusive behavior. I have seen people being held down and tickled until they wet themselves. It's a humiliating experience and can create bitterness in the relationship. **A joke at someone else's expense is rarely funny or helpful.**

I find great pleasure in playing with words and using double meanings and puns. It's a lot of fun and can be quite titillating to flirt with your partner and engage in verbal foreplay. I enjoy a man with a quick wit and great sense of humor. I like to play "word games" with each person returning the verbal volley of the other. Seeing who can create the most interesting innuendo becomes a personal challenge.

Try cultivating a sense of humor through flirtation with your lover. When something really stresses you out find a way to release the stress and laugh it off.

Author's Experience: One day when my son was eight years he had a particularly difficult day at school because someone hit him in the mouth. He had an even worse experience when he wasn't included in an activity with a group that was very important to him because he didn't get a message about a change in the schedule. We decided to make the best of it. I held him, rocked him, and rubbed his feet. We decided to laugh it off by having a pizza and root beer party at home.

As we went to the store, I talked to both of my children about how important it was to learn to do something fun or nice for yourself when you're feeling down and to find a way to get some laughter going. They both accepted this. My daughter (six years old at the time) thought about it a moment and said, **"I think when you laugh you get all of the bad air out, and let the good air in."** I thought this was a great way of explaining the process.

We went home to have our pizza and root beer party. Since most children love to burp and can be quite disgusting at times, we decided that rather than forbid it all the time we would occasionally give them an outlet for their need to be gross. Our house rule was that when we have a pizza and root beer party everyone is allowed to burp at the table and you can't say excuse me. Instead, the response after a great burp is "Good root beer!" It let's off a lot of tension!

Later members of the group who had accidentally left him out, took him for ice cream, and said they we're sorry for the mix-up. They went out of their way to include him after he told them how he felt left out. It has turned into a very rewarding experience because he chose to talk it out and the group has great leaders.

Children are an Endless Source of Enjoyment and Humor

I made it a habit to write down the funny things that my children and younger siblings have said while growing up. Reading them together is a source of fun reminiscing that the children really enjoy. If I had not recorded them at that time I'm sure I would have forgotten most of those precious quotes.

Affirmations

Lesson: I was introduced to affirmations by a massage client and they became a way of life. I used affirmations along with written goals to achieve my major purposes. I had always set goals and had many successes in areas other than personal relationships, so I had a belief that I could trust myself to succeed. I began to study all I could find about healthy, respectful, relationships and effective communication and problem solving. I was determined to change. I had to learn assertive options in my behavior and communications. **Once I determined what I needed and wanted, the resources and knowledge came pouring in.**

> **Application: You can use affirmations to give your mind concise instructions about what to do and what conditions to create in your life.**

How to Make a Good Affirmation:

- Write what you want in the present tense as though it's already a fact, because it will in fact become your reality if you say it frequently and with emotional conviction.

- Fredric Lehrman author of the audio series: "Prosperity Consciousness How to Tap Your Unlimited Wealth", suggests that if you have doubts about the effectiveness of affirmations, start first with the one "All my affirmations work for me whether I believe it or not."

- State affirmations in the positive sense, for example instead of saying, "I never get sick, or I don't get angry," try "I enjoy perfect health," or "I am always in control of my thoughts and emotions."

- After you have the concept that affirmations work firmly in place, you can create many others to help mold and shape your personality and your circumstances or outer realities. Fredric further suggests that if you say an affirmation and find your mind arguing with it, analyze what the objections are and construct an affirmation to deal with those issues. Another brilliant affirmation of his is, "All my past failures have given me a tremendous personal advantage."

I have found affirmations to be the core of my success in overcoming old habits of thought and behavior.

You can use them to great advantage. Take the time to develop some affirmations of your own or use mine (see Appendix B: Life-Improving Affirmations).

Lesson: I used to think I was the most unlucky, persecuted person I knew of. I couldn't believe so many terrible things could happen to one person. Gradually I learned to turn my thinking around 180 degrees. My perspective changed dramatically when I applied this principle of turning things around, which I received as an answer to prayer.

As I began considering the most difficult events of my life, almost like a motion picture events were brought to my remembrance. As I saw the experience from a different perspective a feeling of peace swept over me. I had been driven to my knees emotionally and spiritually in forceful ways because of the magnitude of the difficulties, I encountered.

These precise difficulties were exactly what I needed to seek divine guidance; they helped me discover the principles I'm sharing with you now. While I was very ill and required a lot of bed rest, I had many hours of contemplative time to reflect on my life, to listen to inspiration, and to learn. Ironically, the illness was the cultivating time of my greatest growth. Since that time, I've set aside time daily to do problem solving, meditation, and read inspiring messages.

> **We choose whether our experiences make us better or bitter!**

Application: We always have a choice in our difficulties. We can grow bitter or grow in humility and seek guidance outside of ourselves.

I chose to seek for answers and strength. This is how the Lord can work all things for our good, but only if we acknowledge the purpose of His lessons, instead of simply protesting. *I seriously doubt if I would have had the courage and motivation to change so dramatically if I had not experienced such enormous trials.*

Application: Learn to look at life from another perspective.

I was guided to satisfactory ways to resolve all of my greatest difficulties. Those that I could not change, I learned to reframe through visualization. I also began to look for the lesson and blessings I received from each experience that far outweighed the difficulty in most cases.

One of my affirmations that I constructed after having this life altering change in perspective is, "I am the happiest, most blessed, prosperous person I know," and I mean it!

How many people can actually say that they *know* that the Lord has intervened to preserve their life more than once? I don't know many. Finally, I quit whining about how many times I was brought to the brink of death, and physical assault. As I acknowledged the amazing things that happened to *prevent* it from happening, I felt very blessed to know that the Lord takes an active part in my life and truly cares about what happens to me.

I know that God cares personally about each of us.

My greatest blessing is my indomitable will and resilience. I knew there had to be more to my life than what I had been experiencing. I would not be satisfied with what I was experiencing. I resolved I would change my life for the better, or die trying! For some people, it takes that amount of commitment to begin the healing process.

Inspiration

The Strongest Steels are Refined in the Hottest Fires

We won't know how strong we are until we are subjected to the "fire of adversity". Then you can say with all the conviction of your soul, "I deserve to be happy and experience all the good things in life. I've earned it!"

> **Behold I have refined thee, but not with silver, I have chosen thee in the furnace of affliction.**
>
> **Isaiah 48:10**

Application: When you determine to move forward and change, regardless of the difficulty or the personal cost, you will be assisted in your quest by God, and the universe will be set in motion to assist you in ways you never dreamed possible!

Most often, the Lord uses other good people to assist us along our path. Expect to meet those who will assist you through the wisdom they have gained from their trials.

- Expect to have the resources of health, energy, and wisdom to know what path you should travel next and what pitfalls to avoid along your way.

- Expect to be victorious and triumphant in your quest to refine yourself.

- Give thanks for each step of progress and each act of assistance you receive.

Receive all things with thanks. When we receive all things with thanks, our blessings will be multiplied.

Yes, I had incredible challenges with my health, but I lived! With God's help, I beat death several times. Illness was a time for me to contemplate my life's difficulties and seek direction. It changed my outlook. The Lord used my illness to suit his purposes of refining me.

We are never given a trial that we cannot overcome with the help of God and our own determination. *The strongest spirits are sent to the situations of greatest difficulty because they are able to get through it!* It is a validation of God's trust in you that you have big problems if you have not brought them upon yourself through choices that violate God's Laws.

There are timeless truths that govern the universe and all who live in it. Our disbelief or ignorance to the principles does not change the fact that they exist. We must seek for these truths, live by them, and teach them to others.

I recently heard a man say he couldn't believe that God could cause such suffering as to allow the death of several young children in one family. I was sorry for the man who did not comprehend that our time on the earth is limited and that our perspective of life is so finite. If God sent us to earth, which I believe he did, would he not also have the wisdom to know when it was our time to return to him through death?

It is not your trials or challenges that determine who you are but how you work with them and what you learn from them that matters most. The choice is yours.

Reward Yourself:

Application: When you are working through a trial, it's important to reward yourself with activities that bring you satisfaction and pleasure. These are the things that give you the motivation to keep going. Make a list of things you'd really like to do, and then do them!

- If you like reading, get some Chicken Soup for The Soul books by Mark Victor Hansen and Jack Canfield. They will lift your spirits and renew your determination.

- Involve yourself in activities you enjoy, just for yourself, or with others. Take up a new hobby or pursuit.

- Take a long luxurious bath without any interruptions. Get a massage. Whatever you find pleasurable, take time to do it!

- I have found that I need to create something after I have come to the resolution of a heavy problem. After all the analyzing, I have to use the other side of my brain to create something. So I paint, sew, plant some new plants, or create a flower arrangement. Sometimes it is something else creative like cooking an exotic meal or trying a new recipe.

Keep a "Happy Journal"

I keep a **Happy Journal**—a book with a list of things that make me happy. They are things I can do to make me appreciate the beauty of life. I keep these in a journal that also includes a list of the blessings I acknowledge for that day. I also have written some of the most inspiring quotes I have collected over the years to life my spirits when I'm feeling down. When I'm struggling to find my inner joy, I get out my Happy Journal and read what I'm grateful for and more thoughts of gratitude come. I make sure to do several things from my happy list each day. Usually I begin and end the day with something from this list. It's great to do something for yourself each day that brings you joy, whether you are in crisis or not.

My List includes things to touch all of my senses. Get in touch with yourself and the joy of your senses: Embrace: Touch, Taste, Sight, Sound, and Smell.

Here's an example of my "Happy List":

Aromatherapy	Hot Baths	Soak in the Hot Tub
Flowers	Money	New Clothes
Dancing	Singing	Good Music
Walks in Nature	Sparkling Candlelight	Sounds of Birds
Good Food	Chocolate	Learn something new
Sparkling Lights	Sparkly Jewelry	Jingly Coin Belts/Bellydance
Drums	Bunnies	Bonfires
Hearth Fires	Oceans	Cruises
Cheese	Sunshine	Sewing
Reading	Perfume	Sunsets
Herbal Tea	Massages	Feeling Love
Candlelight Dinners	Time Alone	Movies

In the "Gratitude" pages of my Happy Journal, I write one or two things that I have accomplished and feel a sense of accomplishment about, and I write what I feel grateful for. It doesn't have to be a big deal just something to shift your mind away from what's not working to the things that are. Some of my gratitude entries include:

- "I'm grateful for my home, for shelter emotionally and physically and for variety in my life.

- "I'm grateful for my body, for its beauty, endurance, senses and health."

- "I'm grateful for: Courage, resilience, knowledge, family, friends, learning, growing, talents, children, my body, abundance, employment, respect, the beauty of the earth and faith."

Exercise: Take this space to create your Happy List. Make sure to include at least 20 things and embrace as many senses as possible.

Happy List:	Gratitude List:

Phoenix's Insights and Inspirational Quotes:

- When you're living your life very intentionally, consider than any difficulty that comes to you is a lesson you still need to learn.

- A pearl is what an oyster does with an irritant. What will you do with yours?

- Changing my perspectives allowed me to progress and heal. I learned that when you can make any sense of what has happened or is happening, by seeing the possible benefit, you can resolve it and heal.

- Changing your perspective creates a *new reality*. Even if you haven't changed the circumstances, it changes your feelings and how you respond.

- I found that you get to repeat the experience with slight variations over and over until you learn the lesson you're supposed to gain from it!

- What I had to do to recover was learn how to deal with the trauma/drama in more empowering ways, including changing my perspectives. This is the key to healing and resolution of trauma.

- All the suffering and disappointment of my life have made me a very different person than I designed to be in the beginning. But in the long run, it all worked out!

- I believe the most important qualities are the ability to be adaptable and resilient, and to embrace empowering perspectives.

- Sometimes it's hard in the middle of the muck to see that the adversity is actually leading us to a better path-- Trust The Journey. Believe that universe may actually be colluding to bring you the best things-- that could only come through the process of refinement that happens in adversity.

- Right here, right now, I want you to shift your perspective. Instead of thinking of yourself as hopelessly flawed by trauma, I want you to acknowledge that you are amazing! You are adaptable, and resilient-- because you are still here, and you used your skills to survive.

- The key to healing is TO ENGAGE THE MIND AND BODY TOGETHER because they have spent too much time dissociated by the original trauma. This can actually help to re-write the experience creating a different memory, because it is now a different experience in a new environment.

- If you continue to revisit your trauma without visualizing or embodying a different outcome the brain may interpret it as being re-traumatized over and over, not as a single traumatic event.

- Each of you have had an event, or many, that created disempowering responses in your mind and body. For perspective, keep in mind these immediate survival responses got you through the original trauma alive and served a purpose.

- Instead of living in misery, I developed unshakeable determination to limit the power of the abusive people in my life-- and not just survive, but go from victim into victor.

- My mental toughness was born of pain, injury, suffering, and a determination to heal.

- A belief that you absolutely can change your life into a better, more satisfying one is a vital foundation for your healing and growth.

- Finding a possible benefit to your trauma can help to resolve and heal it. It no longer carries the weight of having wasted or ruined your life.

- When someone is abusing their power, I ask myself, "What kind of personal responsibility and power can I exert over myself to limit the power or coercion being exercise against me?

- I have learned how to evaluate habits of thought that held me in unhealthy patterns of behavior until I could change them into thoughts that serve me well.

- I have a strong desire to create a legacy and help others, not just drag my sorry butt around like a bug that hit the windshield.

- Trauma caused me to become mentally tough and resilient- a tremendous benefit and perhaps my greatest asset.

- The most powerful people in the world are those who choose to control themselves!

Inspirational Quotes and Thoughts

- "A person often meets his destiny on the road he took to avoid it". — Jean de La Fontaine

- "To succeed in life, you need two things: ignorance and confidence." —Mark Twain

- "If one advances confidently in the direction of his dreams, and endeavours to live the life which he has imagined, he will meet with success unexpected in common hours." —Henry David Thoreau

- "The fear of death follows from the fear of life. A man who lives fully is prepared to die at any time." —Mark Twain

- "What you get by achieving your goals is not as important as what you become by achieving your goals." —Henry David Thoreau

- "I know of no more encouraging fact than the unquestionable ability of a man to elevate his life by conscious endeavour." —Henry David Thoreau

- "Our doubts are traitors and make us lose the good we oft might win by fearing the attempt"—William Shakespeare

- "Doubt is uncomfortable, certainty is ridiculous"—Voltaire

- "There is nothing more dreadful than the habit of doubt. Doubt separates people. It is a poison that disintegrates friendships and breaks up pleasant relations. It is a thorn that irritates and hurts; it is a sword that kills."-Buddha

- "The more difficulties one has to encounter, within and without, the more significant and the higher in inspiration his life will be."—Horace Bushnell

- "Do the thing you fear most and the death of fear is certain." —Mark Twain

- "If you suffer, thank God! It is a sure sign that you are alive." —Elbert Hubbard

- "What lies behind us and what lies before us are tiny matters compare to what lies within us." —Ralph Waldo Emerson

- "Whatever words we utter should be chosen with care for people will hear them and be influenced by them for good or ill". —Buddha

- "All misfortune is but a stepping stone to fortune."—Henry David Thoreau

- "Great spirits have always encountered violent opposition from mediocre minds."—Albert Einstein

- "Forgiveness is the fragrance that the violet sheds on the heel that has crushed it." —Mark Twain

- "Keep away from people who try to belittle your ambitions. Small people always do that, but the really great make you feel that you, too, can become great." —Mark Twain

- "Life isn't about finding yourself; it's about creating yourself. So live the life you imagined." —Henry David Thoreau

- "Success in the affairs of life often serves to hide one's abilities, whereas adversity frequently gives one and opportunity to discover them."—Horace

- "It's not the size of the dog in the fight, it's the size of the fight in the dog." —Mark Twain

- "I failed my way to success" — Thomas Edison

- "Press on! A better fate awaits thee." —Victor Hugo

- "Energy and persistence conquer all things." —Benjamin Franklin

- "What would life be if we had no courage to attempt anything?" —Vincent Van Gogh

- "Our greatest glory is not in never falling but in rising every time we fall." — Confucius

- "Let me tell you the secret that has lead me to my goal. My strength lies solely in my tenacity." — Louis Pasteur

- "The mind is everything. What you think, you become." —Buddha

- "Nothing can stop the man with the right mental attitude from achieving his goal; nothing on earth can help the man with the wrong mental attitude." — Thomas Jefferson

- "Experience is the teacher of all things." —Julius Caesar

- "Courage is resistance to fear, mastery of fear – not absence of fear" — Mark Twain

- Walden Pond- "I went to the woods because I wished to live deliberately, to front only the essential facts of life, and see if I could not learn what it had to teach, and not, when I came to die, discover that I had not lived. I did not wish to live what was not life, living is so dear; nor did I wish to practice resignation, unless it was quite necessary. I wanted to live deep and suck out all the marrow of life, to live so sturdily and Spartan-like as to put to rout all that was not life, to cut a broad swath and shave close, to drive life into a corner, and reduce it to its lowest terms, and, if it proved to be mean, why then to get the whole and genuine meanness of it, and publish its meanness to the world; or if it were sublime, to know it by experience, and be able to give a true account of it in my next excursion."—Henry David Thoreau

- "With courage you will dare to take risks, have the strength to be compassionate, and the wisdom to be humble. Courage is the foundation of integrity." —Mark Twain

- "We are all in the gutter but some of us are looking at the stars." — Oscar Wilde

Exercise: Go buy a Happy Journal and begin expanding your happy list, write down your blessings and gratitude and **begin to collect quotes that resonate in your soul and inspire you.**

Live By a Set of Written Values

Making a written set of values to live my life by has been one of my most important accomplishments. I made mine almost in the form of my code of conduct and wrote in the style of affirmations. I took several days of meditation and prayer to prepare it because I understood that it was defining my life and my purpose and I wanted it to be just right. Mine is rather lengthy but personally meaningful and addresses all the areas of my major values and concerns.

Several times when I determined to disengage from a caustic relationship, I wrote a letter and quoted the lines from my Code of Conduct Statement that was applicable to that particular situation.

It has been incredibly helpful not to have to debate and worry about every little issue that comes up because the essence of who I am, in my code of conduct, spells things out pretty clearly. It has acted as a fortifying and steadying force under fire.

My main value in life is in taking personal responsibility and accepting accountability. When I began to really live by the message of my Code of Conduct Statement, life became very clear and I had a sense of personal empowerment like never before.

I suggest that everyone should make a Code of Conduct Statement and live by it. Excerpts from mine are included in Appendix A: Code of Conduct Statement.

In your code of conduct you can define your highest values then form your goals and activities around your highest values.

Personal Calendar

I made a personal monthly calendar on my computer. On the top it lists my major activity priorities, in order of their priority, and the most important relationships. On my calendar I have blocked out time to spend in each category and according to each value. On the bottom is my list of top values. It has been very helpful in helping me to stay clear about my focus. I keep it in a zippered 8-1/2 x11 notebook. I choose this size because I can easily enclose paper from many sources into this book of treasures.

I also took dividers and compiled sections for each of my major areas of focus: Romance, Finance and Wealth, Family, Uplifting Thoughts, Affirmations, Code of Conduct Statement, Roles and Goals, Business, and an area for notes on the current personal development book I'm reading etc.

> **Application: I suggest compiling a similar notebook for yourself even if you have a separate calendar.** It will give your life added direction and clarity. It will help clarify your life purpose and help you get what you really want out of life.

Creating a Positive Influence on Others

Author's Experience: I am keenly aware that the time I have to influence my children and grandchildren is limited. I desire to pass on the things I've learned so that the next generations have the benefit of what I have learned through my hardships- so they don't have to be repeated. I am astounded at how easily they understand and embrace the life lessons that I teach them. I hope that with this foundation, their adult years will be happy and productive and they will be excellent parents. Everything I learned in my life and shared with my children they understood and applied in grade school.

Relationships which used to be the greatest source of sorrow and fear, are now so fulfilling that I am amazed at the depth of joy I feel. I am far more selective about who I engage in with relationships with at any level. I assertively stop others from abusively invading my emotional and physical space. I am more deeply connected to my family and a few choice friends than I ever thought possible.

The things that were so hard to deal with before are much easier now because I think and act differently, and it's working! I learned to express my feelings and needs effectively with the positive expectations that my needs would be met. I learned how to take initiative and get the things I need and want for myself instead of expecting or wishing someone else would do it for me.

Next, I showed my family how to ask for what they want instead of expecting others to guess or just know. I give each of them the opportunity to express their opinions and feelings before I make a decision that concerns them. Although I don't always agree with their perspective, the love between us has grown exponentially *because we feel cared about when we are listened to.*

In my family, we problem solve and negotiate for change all the time. If someone has offended another, "I'm sorry," is always said, not from coercion, but a genuine desire to repair the hurt or offense. We have the confidence that we can talk out and work through any problem or disagreement because we constantly remind each other that our relationship is more important than always getting our own way or being "right".

Often at a family gathering or dinner with my adult children, we exchange compliments with each person. We each have the opportunity but are not coerced into sharing something we appreciate or admire about our loved one, or compliment them on something they have worked hard to achieve.

We try to be supportive of what each family member is working to achieve in their life at that time. We give service to each other out of love and respect.

Positive Touch is such an important part of being supportive that we offer supportive hugs to feel each other's positive energy and love. However, it is never forced if someone doesn't feel like it that day. A Hug is the bridge between two people.

My Essential Rights and Boundaries

- You have the right to ignore and repel negativity and unfair criticism.

- You have the right to feel and express your own feelings, whatever they may be.

- You have the right to ask for others to change their behavior when it interferes with your boundaries, and negatively impacts you, or endangers you.

- You have the right to defend yourself emotionally, spiritually, and physically.

- You have the right to learn new ways of thinking and interpreting the circumstances in your life, which thereby causes you to change your mind.

- You have the right to "reframe" your history and interpret it in more useful and empowering ways.

- You have the right to *change*: Your mind, your attitude, your relationships, your job, your religion, your friends, and where you live.

- You have the right to only take responsibility for your own problems, and not to solve another's problems for them.

- You have the right to do anything that is good and assists you in making empowering progress.

- You have the right to be treated with kindness and respect.

- You have the right to say No to requests that violate your boundaries, ethics, or just don't feel right.

- You have the right to privacy in your thoughts, feelings, and environment.

- You have the right to experience exquisite JOY!

- You have the right to forgive—If and when YOU feel like it. Not when others say you should.

- You have the right to get help and support when you need it.

- The other person's rights end where yours begin.

Remember, you alone are responsible for what you think, say and do.

Learn To Be Assertive in All Your Interactions

Author's Experience- Once I learned how to quit being a doormat and become assertive my life is much more rewarding. It's astounding how much more effective I am now. Some people aren't sure how to handle it because they're not used to anyone being so straightforward and direct. In a conflict, it's disarming to them because I say exactly what I want and expect as the outcome, without being angry and threatening. I don't push my way around but when someone has obviously violated my rights or my trust in them, I confront them directly so it can be resolved.

An example occurred when I went to a doctor's appointment for a checkup. I took my young daughter with me who was also sick and had an appointment with her doctor shortly after mine. While in the room waiting for the doctor to enter, I needed a drink so I got a paper cup from the dispenser and helped myself to a drink from the sink. My daughter watched and also wanted a drink. I told her she could get one. About this time the doctor came in and began asking me routine questions about my health.

As my daughter reached over to get a cup from the dispenser to get a drink, he reached out to grab her arm to prevent her from getting a cup, then he stopped himself before he actually grabbed her. He said to me "She doesn't need a drink, there's already a cup on the counter!" I replied the cup was mine and we weren't sharing germs since she was sick and was going to the doctor after my appointment with him. (She had a very stuffed nose and had been forced to breathe through her mouth causing a dry mouth and had a legitimate need for a drink of water.) He was highly agitated and my child was so afraid of his obvious anger that she came over and sat beside me and buried her face behind me. I was really mad that he had intimidated her so much over a stupid cup that couldn't cost more than five cents.

I left the appointment and began to look for a new doctor. When I had confirmed an appointment with another doctor, I cancelled my follow up visit with that doctor. **I surprisingly had the occasion to meet him in the hall of the medical building the next day.** I asked to speak to him for a moment. He stopped in the hall and I told him how unhappy I was at the way he had treated my young daughter. He replied that she was distracting him. I said "Maybe so, but you had no right to intimidate her by acting like you were going to grab her arm and prevent her from getting a cup. He said, "Well I didn't grab her arm." I told him it was a really good thing he hadn't because there would be some serious ramifications for it. Since this was just one of countless experiences with him and his staff where I was treated with rudeness and insensitivity, I left and never returned to his office. I don't have to tolerate this type of treatment and I let my daughter know that I had changed doctors after he treated her that way. She had told me *she didn't ever want to go to any doctor again*, which is an understandable reaction for a five year old. My defense of her being mistreated helped her to change her mind and she has had a few pleasant doctors since then.

Application: I have totally quit enabling the misuse of power no matter where it comes from. You should too!

Learn to be assertive by expressing your feelings and needs and by not allowing others to mistreat you.

Let people know when they have offended you—**then let it go!** Don't continue to rehearse it in your mind. Learn to forgive. There is a huge difference in forgiving someone and allowing the mistreatment or abuse to continue. This understanding was a crucial breakthrough for me. I had to learn that sometimes "turning the other cheek" really hurts all involved. **When you enable abuse, no one is benefited!**

I trust myself to conquer any problem that I am faced with by applying the same principles I have learned through the painful processes I have encountered. I see how sharing my perspective with others helps them to see their own problems more clearly and look for solutions instead of staying stuck in their misery.

I feel the guiding hand of a loving God who leads me from one situation to another that has new information vital to solving my problems. I recognize that the only people without problems are dead people. So I just keep learning and moving forward. I don't feel like I'll ever be finished sculpting my own work of art that is myself. As I encounter difficulties, I think of how they polish off the rough edges of my life.

Effective Communication and Negotiation
Learn How to Get Your Needs Met Through Assertive Communication

Learn assertive ways of communication. One way of doing this is to express yourself through a "Structured Request for Change" that shows you are taking responsibility for your own feelings and not blaming anyone else. It allows you to state the behavior you object to or would like changed, how it affects you, and ask for a change and possibly tell them what you will do to counteract their behavior if they don't make a change.

It gives you an opportunity to clearly state what your feelings are about someone else's behavior in the least hostile way. This is a basic form of assertive communication in which you take responsibility for your own feelings; and request a change while recognizing that the other person may not change. The pioneer of the "I-message" is Thomas Gordon. *You may have to figure out a way to get your needs met in another way without their cooperation.*

The basic components of a "Structured Request for Change" are:

- Tell the person what they did that you would like them to change.

- Tell them how you feel about their behavior and how it negatively affects you.

- Ask them politely to change their behavior.

- Discuss possible consequence—**or what you will do for yourself**, if they don't meet your polite request to change their behavior.

- Stating a consequence is optional and not always necessary. It's helpful with children, and any time you have already made a polite request that's been ignored.

- It may be to your advantage, or more empowering, to simply ask for change and if it doesn't occur **show that you can go around their behavior** to get your needs met in another way.

- This is particularly helpful when you are dealing with an abusive individual who may interpret you statement of what you are going to do if they don't change their behavior as a threat. Sometimes it's better to just do what you need to do to get around them.

Some examples of this type of structured request for change messages are:

- When I need to assert myself to a client who missed their massage appointment without any notice: "When you miss your appointment without giving me 24 hours notice, I feel frustrated because I don't have the ability to fill that time with someone else who needs the help, and it costs me money. Next time, please give me 24 hours notice or I may have to charge you for the missed appointment."

- When a person is heatedly venting their anger or frustration at you: "When you yell and swear at me I feel threatened and upset. It makes me feel like I don't want to talk to you. When you can talk to me without yelling and swearing, I'd really like to work this out with you. Can we schedule a time to work on this?"

- A spouse to another spouse: "When you expect me do to all of the housework without giving me a hand, I feel taken advantage of. I'm tired from working all day too. Will you give me a hand with the dishes? If I don't get more help I may have to hire a maid."

- A lover to their loved one: "When you don't take time to talk to me about what's important to me, or hold me in a meaningful way, I feel ignored, and unimportant to you. Can we set aside 5 minutes each day for meaningful touch and talk?"

Give a Really Meaningful Compliment

Use this same style when giving a compliment. With a slight modification of this structured message technique you can affirm or compliment someone in a meaningful way.

- State what you like about their behavior, or personality, or something else you appreciate about them.

- State how you feel about any of those things.

- Add something about how it affects you if appropriate.

Examples of compliments or positive affirming statements

Spouse to spouse: "When you slipped a love note under my pillow I felt surprised and cared for. Thank you for your thoughtfulness."

Parent to child: "I can see you have really been keeping the family room cleaner. I feel good knowing you're taking more responsibility around the house. It makes my job a lot easier. Thanks."

Employer to employee: "I really appreciate you getting that document prepared so quickly. I was able to get the bid out on time today. It's nice to have an employee I can count on!"

Nurturing Positive Relationships

Create Bonding with Compliments

Relationships are the key to real happiness! Spend time individually with your children, spouse or, if you are single, with your close friends. There are little opportunities daily to compliment your family and friends, and check in to see how they are doing and feeling.

At your evening meal take time to offer compliments before eating the meal. A more formal approach to keep your family close is to have a special individual "interview" time for each of your children. At this meeting give them the opportunity to discuss current events in their lives, calendar when they need your help with transportation and assist them in setting goals for themselves.

Take the time to offer specific compliments tailor-made for each person and make suggestions about how they might enhance certain areas to help the family or their own life run more smoothly. Together set short and long-term goals. If the child has some goals that are too personal to share, they can record them in a diary or journal. This individual time with each family member is a strong form of bonding.

Create Ground Rules for Resolving Conflict

In my family and personal relationships the underlying factors are "We talk out our problems." *The relationship is more important than the argument*, whatever it is, and we have the skills to work it out to a successful conclusion.

- You must be respectful in your tone of voice while telling your side of the argument. This includes the adults speaking to the children.

- Each person has a chance to express their feelings, and tell their side of the story. If a person cannot get past the anger to discuss things rationally and logically, they are excused and encouraged to go do something to "get the anger out."

- No one is allowed to ridicule, or insult another person. We stick to the issue at hand and don't dig up a lot of old history because we deal with things as they come up instead of letting them fester.

- If a problem comes up we deal with it immediately. "The schedule" is dropped and an attempt is made to solve the problem then and there. If it doesn't reach a successful conclusion immediately, we set up a time agreed upon by all members to try it again.

- Finally: All need to acknowledge what their part of the problem is, however small it may be.

- **Examine any possible benefits that have come from the conflict**, maybe it's a greater understanding or yourself or the other person, or the opportunity to change instead of causing irreparable damage to the relationship!

Apologies Heal

"I'm sorry" cannot be used just to get things over with or to manipulate the other person. If it can't be sincere, skip it. It is often appropriate even when you don't own the problem to say, "I'm sorry that you feel that way, I still love you" or "I'm sorry this has happened, I'd like to work this out." Saying I am sorry doesn't mean you are wrong, or the person taking the blame, it means you are adult enough to put the relationship above the need to right or in control of the other.

We end a conflict by some form of physical bonding, a hug, a kiss, a hand massage, foot rub, or back rub. It's critically important to re-establish the touch connection. Nothing says, "I accept you," more effectively than appropriate touch.

> **The two most important words for healing wounded feelings are "I'm sorry," but only when the tone of voice and intent is sincere.**

Sincere Apologies Must Be Spoken In The Way They Feel Loved

When someone offends another by deliberately or unintentionally doing something hurtful, or by disregarding a boundary or agreement, **psychic wounds are created** and emotional distance between the two people is inevitable. There are many ways we can be offended. The most important thing to heal the wound is a sincere apology.

In my religion we believe the steps to repentance when you have sinned or wronged another are: Acknowledgement of the transgression, Remorse for the problem, Make Restitution to the offended, Ask for forgiveness from the offended, and very importantly—Try to never do it again!

These same elements can be used when apologizing. **If you make restitution by trying to communicate in that person's way of showing affection, the person will feel the apology is sincere.** *For a verbally oriented person*, saying "I'm really sorry", and following up with a love letter stating all the things you love and appreciate about that person will go a long way toward healing the wound. *For a task-oriented person*, ask, "What can I DO to make this right?" They will probably want a specific action or maybe a gift acknowledging how much you care about them. *For a physically oriented person*, the restitution likely needs to involve some loving touch, either from the offender, or give them a gift certificate to get some pampering or nurturing at a spa or with a massage. Again, the idea is to make restitution in a way that's meaningful and sincere to THEM, not how you think they should "get over it!"

Become an Expert Communicator

When you encounter a problem look at it as an opportunity to teach others about your needs, rights, expectations, and desire to change the world for good. It is also an opportunity to learn about the other person's needs, feelings, and values. **After listening to their point of view, your position on an issue may change.**

> **Application: Practice effective communication**. Use structured feeling messages for compliments and requests for change.
>
> **In a conflict, address the *feelings* of each person *before* attempting to resolve it.** If the feelings are not dealt with first, it will be difficult, if not impossible, to come to a successful resolution of the problem.

People want to know you care about their feelings too, not just your own. Use structured messages to express your feelings, state the problem, and give possible solutions to resolving the issue. If you use this structure for confronting, you won't insert a lot of unneeded information. You can stick to the point and feel reasonably in control of your emotions. Then if the other person gives you a sincere "I'm sorry" and makes an effort to improve, it's worth engaging in the effort to continue to work on a relationship with them.

Examples of some effective openers for conflict resolution are:

- What would make this feel better?
- What do you need from me to make this situation better?
- What do you want from me right now?
- What do you see as my part in this problem?
- What can I do to heal the wound between us?
- If we could work together and get to the best possible outcome for you, what would that look and feel like to you? (Get them to describe their best possible outcome.)
- Will you tell me what you need and I'll see if I can meet any of those needs.

When they can clarify their needs you're both in a position to immediately get to some resolution or at least learn if you can get to a place of having each person's needs met. Each person needs the opportunity to be heard and state what they need so the individuals can see *if and where* they can come together and solve the issue at hand. This saves SO MUCH TIME! Instead of meandering through a lot of peripheral nonsense you can get right to the point.

If you attempt to resolve a difficulty in a relationship with another person and you state your needs and they agree to meet them but continually engage in the behavior that feels destructive or dishonoring to you, you may need to disengage permanently from the relationship to take care of your own needs.

If the person you are trying to work things out with has an abusive or toxic personality you may never get an apology or you may get one meant to simply pacify you.

A very typical response from a person with an abusive nature is an elaborate, seemingly sincere apology. *Or they may just make promises of change that never materialize.* As soon as the victim is lulled into passivity by promises of change, the abuser is "off the hook" and resumes the old behavior. It may only be a few hours before they have abandoned their promise to change or stop. This can go on in an endless cycle. *The bottom line is to insist that they take personal responsibility for their actions and look for real changes in their behavior.*

If insistence that they own their bad behavior escalates to aggression—LEAVE.

> **Application: I have observed that people will treat you just about how you expect to be treated. Toxic people will push you just as far as you let them.**

We have the right to be treated with respect, and caring. We have the right to have our feelings heard. It's our responsibility to show and tell others how we want to be treated. We also have to act the way we want to be treated so that they have a desire to treat us respectfully in return.

In a relationship, work toward healthy interactions and give them a reasonable chance to change, if they don't want to engage in a healthy exchange, move along!

> **I don't believe in participating in relationships that are deeply destructive—no matter who the relationship is with.**

Families present a special case for this commitment. We don't just give up on them whimsically. Hopefully, we become families to love, nurture, and help each other to develop into the best person we can become.

When deeply abusive or destructive patterns are present in family dynamics, it's harder to determine when and how to terminate a familial relationship. I don't believe anyone has the right to violate another, emotionally, physically, or spiritually.

I believe in the intrinsic ability that each of us has to change and reach for a higher level of being. This is the essence of my message. Sometimes it takes the termination of a significant relationship or family bond to stop the pattern of abuse. It may be the only catalyst strong enough to help them make the necessary changes in themselves. *You may be the only one courageous enough to break the chains of abuse, perhaps from generations before. It's worth it!*

When one person refuses to negotiate, compromise, or remain faithful to their commitments, relationships fail. With abuse, the abuser is denying the needs and feelings of the victim to selfishly gratify his or her own feelings or needs. When a person refuses to change or accept advice or counsel that would improve the relationship, the root is still selfishness. It takes continued effort from both partners to make a loving, successful relationship. The same goes for a parent child relationship once the child reaches a reasonable age of maturity. It's worth every effort to make it work—but only if both people are working together.

If a destructive relationship takes place outside the family, why tolerate it? Get out and make a change. Actually, it usually needs to happen the other way around. You have to change the pattern in *yourself* that is allowing the other person to mistreat you. Otherwise, you will repeat the pattern of destructive relationships. The best place to learn to stand up for yourself and make the changes needed is in a difficult or abusive relationship.

Learn to tell others what you will and will not tolerate, give them a chance to respond appropriately. If they will not, find a new job, a new teacher, a new friend, new partner, etc. Quit enabling unhealthy and destructive patterns in relationships!

We can learn this lesson in a variety of circumstances. The point is you must learn the lesson or it will be continually recycled until you do. For example: I needed to learn how to assert myself and how to enforce appropriate boundaries, effective conflict resolution, develop a knowledge of my true worth, and draw upon my personal power. **Jenny** had to learn to terminate caustic relationships and to defend herself physically and emotionally. **Holly** had to learn how to problem-solve like an adult and see avenues she did not know were open to her in making choices. She had to overcome her despair and focus on what she wanted instead of what she was presently experiencing.

The Lord does not expect us to endure the abusive exercise of others people's agency. "Turning the other cheek" in an abusive relationship can get you killed—Really! This was perhaps the hardest lesson for me to learn. I urge you to learn to distinguish between the relationships that are beneficial and the ones that are toxic and give yourself permission to leave the toxic ones.

> **I believe that each of us has been given specific circumstances in life that will be the best means for learning what is really important and necessary for us individually.**

Quit Rewarding and Enabling Bad Behavior and Misuse Of Power

If you have been given poor service or treated rudely, make a point to say something about it to the person in charge. Imagine how you would feel as a business owner pouring your lifeblood and energy into your business only to have it undermined, or even destroyed, by uncaring and rude employees. It may give the employer an opportunity to correct the behavior so that their business is preserved and the next patron will have a more pleasant experience. In addition, the employee has a chance to learn some vital skills about personal relationships that will help them to get along better in society.

In general, when asking for a change in behavior, first tell the offender what behavior you are objecting to. Then explain how you felt about their actions, and its possible

effects on your business or life. Finally, tell them what you want and expect. If you only tell them what you didn't like, their minds tend to gravitate toward it and they may repeat the behavior, although they are trying not to. Make sure to end the conversation with someone you are confronting with the exact instructions or expectations of what you want him or her to do. This is what will stay in their minds.

A polite request will get you further than chewing someone out. If you point out the negative impact of their behavior, most people are courteous enough to be motivated to change. Afterward, make sure to notice what they are doing right. Any effort toward positive change must be acknowledged and verbally rewarded. In essence, tell them "Don't do that, do this instead."

- For example, an employer could say: "When you ignored that customer and then argued with them when they asked you for help, it cost me their business. Next time, even if you are busy, look up and tell them you will be right with them and give them a smile. Then when you can get to them, give them your full attention. Treat them like they're our best customer." *Then get agreement from the employee.* "Will you do that?" Wait until they commit to trying before moving on to something else.

Go out of your way to reward good service and friendly behavior! Compliment the person directly and tell their employer or superior. "I really liked the service I got from ________. He or she is a real asset to your company."

Write a thank you, or fill out a comment card.

- Patronize businesses that are exercising a superior work ethic with friendly, courteous, service. You'll be amazed at the difference you feel in your life when you do this. There is far less stress and you are actually making progress in making our environment a better place. People tend to perform at your level of expectation of them. What you acknowledge and affirm tends to get repeated.

Written Goals Get Things Done!

Share with your family what you are working on in your life as well. Or maybe you want to choose and accountability partner to share your goals with. A strong example of goal setting will firmly establish the habit for your children and will benefit generations to come. You can also set up a reward system or some form of acknowledgement of each goal achieved.

I use goals and sub-goals, long and short-term goals and affirmations to help reinforce my goals. I have included a form on goals and affirmations that I used when my young children were young in Appendix D: Goals & Affirmations. You can copy it or adapt it for your own use.

Here's how to use the chart. Make a list of list of 100 or more goals. Choose five that are top priority in various areas of focus; for example, Business, Social, Family, Emotional, Physical, Financial, Spiritual, Personal Development, and Educational. It's important to have goals in a variety of areas to stay well balanced and to enjoy your life to the fullest. If your goal is to exercise four times a week for 15 minutes a day, write it down on the lines on the left side of the chart. Each day that you accomplish that goal write "Yes!, Triumph!, or Victory!" in the corresponding daily box.

For younger children, let them help choose their goals and reward each day of achievement with a special sticker. To make it easier to accomplish these goals reinforce it with an affirmation that you say to yourself several times a day. For example affirm something like: "I enjoy working out. I am enjoying all the benefits of perfect health. It's easy for me to nurture and care for my body properly"

Make one or more affirmations for each goal. Affirmations should be written as though you have already achieved the goal and they are a statement of fact. Restate the affirmations aloud frequently. It's estimated that it takes 21 days to form a new habit. You will probably want to repeat some goals for three or more weeks. Some goals may be short term and you may want to write them down and acknowledge them as soon as they're accomplished. You can take time for about 15 minutes each day to relax, close your eyes and visualize yourself achieving your goals. Think of as many details as you can about how it will feel and be when you have achieved this goal.

When you see yourself through visualization in your mind as though the goal is already achieved, and hear yourself stating that you have already achieved your goal, and you visually track your progress toward your goal with this charting system, you have a very powerful tool for getting exactly what you want!

Application: Some people believe in setting concise, realistic goals so that you can achieve systematic definable results. Others believe you should set completely unrealistic goals—lots of them. Make hundreds of goals, maybe even thousands for each area of focus in your life. This theory is if you don't dream big, you'll never get the incredible results you can get by setting unrealistic goals. The difference between a big unrealistic dream and one that comes true is your belief that you can do it and consistent work toward that big dream. The unrealistic, big dreams become realistic because of the power of our subconscious mind to draw to us what we think about.

How to Set Clear, Concise Goals

Decide what you want then write it down and outline exactly how you plan to get it. The more specific you can be the easier it will be to get it. When you write something down it's like making a commitment to yourself instead of just wishing. It helps to set a target date for the achievement of your goal. Keep the list of your goals and your accomplishments to give you a boost when you feel discouraged. You can look back at all of your achievements and feel that you can do anything because you have already proven your ability to set and achieve goals. Throughout the year I make and keep lists of the goals I have achieved. It's amazing to look back and concisely see where I have been. You forget that you were struggling once you have met the goal. It's a real boost to see your progress on paper.

Author's Experience: I set out a clear plan of what I wanted and the action steps to get there. It shaped my life and although there were some minor deviations, I have lived the game plan and I'm receiving rich rewards and enjoyment that would not be possible if I had not learned to be assertive and stand up for my personal freedoms.

Change can be very frightening and feel threatening, but if you trust in your ability to get through anything and God's willingness to assist you, you will make great changes.

When I made monumental changes in the dynamics of my relationships with others, I felt like I was jumping off a cliff with no parachute. God would either catch me or I would end up a bloody mess at the bottom.

God caught me and He will catch you too, if you are doing your part with everything you have!

Selfishness is the Primary Cause for Failure in Relationships

When you put your needs, feelings and wants consistently ahead of the other person's it builds resentment, hostility, conflict, and may destroy the relationship!

Happy Relationships

As I healed and decided to engage in healthier relationships, I realized I had a lot to learn. I devoured all the information I could find on happy relationships. Then I took a careful assessment of my own and realized forcefully that I had an unhealthy intimate relationship. When I ended the relationship and became single, I took the time to listen to and read a lot of material on healthy relationships and how to get over a significant break-up. It was very cleansing. I looked at it as a time of rebirth for me.

Many of my closest confidants in life are men. They seem to have the ability to cut through the nonsense and see things more objectively and clearly than women in general. I wanted to get together with some male friends because I find their perspective refreshing. I genuinely enjoy male companionship.

I thought about what characteristics I liked about myself and what I wanted to accentuate. I thought about what my major objectives were in an intimate relationship.

One of the key principles I discovered in my reading is that some women love too much by giving up their own happiness for their partner's especially if they have been abused in the past.

> **Another key principle that really resonates with me is that we are attracted to the people who have some element in their lives or personalities that represents unfinished business in our lives.**

We are drawn to the people who will help us resolve our unfinished issues. If the person you bond with is also invested in learning, healing and growing themselves; you are in the best possible place to work out your "stuff."

If you partner with someone who remains stuck in their patterns, you often see the dynamics you found in your home or past relationships repeating itself. In the final analysis, a relationship is healthy, nurturing and beneficial when both partners are growing together in their individual paths. If the growing stops, or only one partner wants to progress, the relationship will sour and become unhealthy. When this happens, however painful it is, your own growth and happiness depends on your courage to continue growing by ending that relationship. This principle is as true for friendships as it is for marriages.

The best chance for you to get what you want out of your relationship is to know what you want in the first place and be willing to continually work toward your own growth while learning and exploring the other person's needs. Ultimately, we are responsible to make sure our own needs are met and not demand that someone else meet them.

Another crucial element in a healthy relationship is your willingness to be vulnerable with each other. Do you approach the relationship with a need to protect or a willingness to learn about your partner and their needs? Growth and true emotional and sexual intimacy only come when you drop your defenses and interact with your partner with the intent to learn. Regardless of the situation, whether it's a conflict or exploring their needs and desires, open, honest discussion of the other's needs, wants and feelings will bring bonding. Together you can more fully achieve your desires when you work together from the intent to learn.

Here is how I define my needs and highest values in a marriage relationship. Some apply to my requirements in a friendship as well.

- I relate to the world predominantly through touch and verbalization. I love to communicate and I have a high need for nurturing touch. I also believe that everyone needs positive touch and that our society is suffering dramatically from touch deprivation. I need a man who knows the difference between nurturing and sexual touch and wants a lot of both.

- I have suffered enormous sorrow and want to have joy and lightheartedness. Everything can get so heavy and serious in my life. A good sense of humor is near the top on my list because I love the playful side of life and a good verbal volley is delicious fun to me.

- Communication is the next most important thing. I rarely communicate on a superficial level because I find it trivial when there is so much need to connect on deeper levels. **People are starving to connect with what's real and important.** The only way to find out what's real and important to them is to talk about it and risk self-disclosure. If you are going to be a confidante of mine, I insist on mutual disclosure. I despise the deception that goes on in many relationships. I value a man who opens up to me, and shares his reality—his hopes, fears, mistakes, and triumphs. I also require this of a close friendship. I figure my time is valuable, I don't know how much of it I have left, and each moment is precious. I resent someone wasting my time with "head games"—the hide and seek so prevalent in relationships. If you are mature and confident enough to disclose your real self, we can play. If not, you should just keep moving.

- I also want a man who contributes to the relationship as a peer. I like to be on the same playing field.

- Sometimes people try to form attachments to me, a quasi-friendship, that seem intent on extracting the life essence out of me with their problems that they refuse to take responsibility for. I have finally given myself permission to extricate myself from whiners—I got a "whinerectomy". I believe friendships need to emotionally nourish and benefit both people. I will help anyone with a genuine desire to take responsibility and make changes, but I don't have the time or energy to engage in relationships that are not mutually nourishing.

- I need a man who is not threatened by a woman with intelligence, a drive to excel, and an indomitable will. I have worked so hard to overcome my passiveness and define and recreate myself and I need someone who can deal with an assertive woman without feeling intimidated. This seems like the hardest requirement to fill. I dated many guys before I committed to a serious long-term relationship, The major reason that most didn't work out was that they were intimidated by me in some way—my intelligence, my achievements, my looks, or my spunk. I felt I had to compromise something in order to be accepted. That was my biggest mistake ever! I tried to change myself into something that compromised the essence of my best qualities in order to be accepted. I know how it feels to live that way and I will never do it again. It was not worth it!

> **Application: Re-define yourself:** The most important thing to remember is that whatever your experiences have been up until now, you can re-program and systematically change anything and everything you want to with consistent, determined effort, goals, positive affirmations, and visualizations. Specialized bodywork (a specific kind of massage designed to release trauma from the body) can assist to release any trauma or unconscious sabotage mechanisms you may have experienced in the past. This is a system that works! I am a living example of how successful this method is.

Define What You Want in a Partner

Make a list of what you want in your Ideal Partner. What are the qualities in your ideal partner? Write them down, even if you're currently married, and share them with your spouse. It can help you re-prioritize where your relationship is going and bring more satisfaction to your life.

> **Application: Make a written list of what you want in your life and in your relationships. Prioritize their values for yourself.**

If you are married, ask your spouse to do the same. Have them prioritize their list. Make a written plan of action with the steps you will take to become closer together in your needs and values. Determine what intermediate steps or actions you need to take for the relationship to be mutually satisfying. Act on your plan immediately to show your commitment to making your lives happier and more satisfying.

Jenny's Experience: "I gained the courage to get out of abusive relationships by reading books on domestic violence and abuse. I read several books about domestic violence and abuse and their effect on the children in these homes. It was very clear that my children and I would not do better by staying in the abusive situation.

One of the key points I learned is that abuse escalates with time and with each successive generation until someone is courageous enough to stop it. Because I had already had my life threatened on several occasions, I was very fearful about what my children would have to deal with. Statistically, my children would grow up and repeat the pattern they saw and lived. I didn't want them to grow up to be abusers or 'doormats.' I also learned to recognize that the behavior of the abusers in most cases follows a predictable pattern—the modus operandi of an abuser. I learned to step out of it as a victim and look at it from a different perspective. **This allowed me to realize that there are some rights and wrongs in relationship behaviors! It was not just my opinion that I was being abused and mistreated.** I learned that there were professionals that recognize and speak out against the behaviors I was continually subjected to. It was incredibly empowering! Now I didn't go through an internal civil war each time I was abused and the perpetrator turned the situation around and blamed me for their abuse."

I had spent years thinking that they had as much right to their opinions and actions as I did. Someone else had to draw the line for me and help me realize I was right in protesting this kind of treatment. I recognized from years of being abused that the seduction of promised changes from an abuser rarely results in positive change. The more I got sucked in to the cycle of abuse and the perpetrator's promises to change, the worse it got.

> **I also learned that before you leave an abusive relationship or a pattern of relating, you had better change yourself or you will simply repeat the pattern in another relationship or in another way but with the same circumstances.**

I also started to open up a little bit with some close friends. I spent years in fear I would accidentally "spill my guts" and tell someone what kind of life I really had. I was afraid of being hurt if the abusers found out. I was equally afraid of not being believed. The most abusive people in my life had a lot of charisma, and were very liked and accepted in our social circles. After sharing only a few details of my personal hell with a few selected friends their feedback helped me see that what I was experiencing was not "normal"! In fact, I had someone comment to me, "With just the few things you've told me about the way you have been treated, I'm surprised you're not an axe murderer!" I know that some women build up enough rage from abuse that they strike out in violence. I'm really opposed to that."

> **Application: Jenny could also help herself heal by visualizing herself as confident, safe, and able to defend herself—both verbally and physically.**

She could visualize herself enjoying nurturing and healthy relationships. She could learn to tune in to her body and its needs and to imagine herself being fully alive in every part of her body. *She could effectively siphon off of all her anger through physical action like a punching bag or a bat against a pillow or bed.* Most importantly, she could learn to listen to her inner voice that could warn her of imminent danger, or possible solutions to her problems.

Fill your mind and days with positive thoughts and timeless truths. It's a key to happiness.

I believe prayer is an essential process in our progression and crucial in turning our trials into triumphs. I firmly believe our prayers are answered. It may not be exactly what we expected, but it will be what we need.

Life Balance Through Supportive, Loving Relationships

Find the Love of Your Life-and Keep Them

Define yourself—seek ultimate understanding of your own needs, desires, attitudes, talents, and your most important values. If you know yourself, you will know what you want in a partner. In the past, I relied heavily on physical attraction as the initial basis for a relationship. In fact, it was commonly voiced in my home of origin that, "If they don't make your 'bum hum' the first time you meet them it will never work.

I was told by my parents that physical attraction is the most important factor in marriage. That is what I believed. After some disastrous relationships (and since I was blowing up my personality) I started questioning everything, including that "sage advice." I began asking the very few friends I knew who had very loving marriages, if they fell immediately in love and had strong physical attraction first, or friendship first. *Without exception, they all said they were friends first.* This was a very novel idea to me. How could that passion grow in you if you don't have it from the beginning? I really didn't know the answer but I was willing to explore another way.

I believe it's vitally important to learn about values, attitudes, and aspirations of your friends and potential partners before you jump in to intimacy. Establish *emotional* intimacy first.

If you don't get to know someone very well before you fall in love, you miss a lot of important details that seem very significant later when you are married to them. Why not get to know all you can about them right from the start? Then if the pieces fit and complement each other, real love has a chance to bloom.

> **It's dangerous to your happiness to wait to find out about the other person's deepest values and feelings until after you have fallen in love and then, with glazed eyes of love, try to make them fit your fantasy of a mate.**

> **Application: Define who you are clearly before you try to find a match or a mate. It will save you a lot of pain.**

The likelihood of you finding the love of your life greatly increases if you have a clear understanding of who you are and what you want. You can then attract to yourself the person with the characteristics that you understand and value. It's been said that anyone can work out a relationship, even if you have opposite characteristics. That may be true, but how much effort has to be expended just to find common ground and a basis for understanding?

A great relationship can be described as a "gem with many facets." Each needs attention and special care or it will become worn and dull. With a balance in each facet of a relationship, it shines and is a thing of beauty for everyone involved. As a couple you have to define what the facets of your relationship are and make sure that each is receiving the time and attention it needs to stay balanced and sparkling.

> **Application: If you haven't found a mate and would like to, I suggest you let go of your intense search and work on loving yourself for a while.**

One of my clients who was single and lamenting over the prospects of ever finding the right woman, said some of the women he met were so intense it was repulsive. He said, "Desperation is a most unattractive perfume!" What a brilliant way to describe the palpable intensity and desperation that some people exude.

Quit worrying about finding "the one" and start making yourself into "the one" that you are meant to be. Then relax with the confidence that if it's the best thing for you, you will find a mate. Your chances of finding a great relationship increase as you approach it relaxed and playfully. How many times have you heard about a couple trying to have a child and after years of disappointment they begin the adoption process only to find out she is pregnant. *When you relax your intensity, more possibilities can open up. Sometimes less is more.*

If You are Already Married, Show Them They are the Love of Your Life!

Together define what the facets of your gem are and if they have become worn and dull, spend some time polishing them. There is a reason you married in the first place. It's worth the effort to make your gem shine.

Find out what it really means to say "I love you" to your partner. Just as we each learn essentially or mostly through one of three avenues; either through sight—visual, through sound—auditory, or through touch or hands on exposure—kinesthetic, these styles of relating to the world carry over to the way we communicate our feelings. They strongly correlate to how we give and receive love. It can be very helpful to know how your mate relates to the world through these avenues. You must also know how you relate to the world. This also applies to how we give and receive apologies.

For the person who relates best through touch: Perhaps the most loving thing you could do is to show love is through some form of touch—a back rub, sensual kissing, or "the full course". They may enjoy public displays of affection. Just stay "in touch" with them and they will feel emotionally satisfied. Touch them when you communicate, and make love as often as possible to make them feel loved and appreciated. If you also communicate through touch that's great, you understand the desire to be touched.

For the person who is more visual or detail-oriented: Maybe the most loving thing you could do is complete a task that they want help with, or one that they hate or one that they clearly can't do for themselves. Perhaps a clean orderly garage would make them feel very loved and appreciated. They see love as "doing"—things like helping with work or giving a present. Ask them to make a list of things they would consider most loving.

For the person who relates to the world predominantly through sound or verbal communication: They want to hear "I love you" a lot. They appreciate any verbal expression of love, affection, or compliments. They particularly enjoy flirtation and "verbal foreplay"—and "afterplay." Talking about love and romance is very important to some people. Many enjoy love letters and "intellectual intercourse" or a meeting of the souls (or bodies) through words. These people particularly like to be heard, so listen attentively.

> **Application: Make a list of things that mean "I love you" and "I appreciate you," for both you and your partner.**

Keep it for future reference and little loving acts of kindness. It may be quite revealing to see the differences or similarities in your list no matter how much you thought you understood each other. *Periodically do something on your mate's list of things that communicates love to them.*

If you are contemplating re-marriage, I strongly suggest talking to people who know your potential spouse very well. If there is a former spouse, and it's appropriate, you should consider contacting them as well. Ask them to please be candid about what their marriage was like. Interview your fiancée's friends, children, parents, and siblings.

Touch and Talk Go Together

I've learned in the many years as a licensed massage practitioner that people will share their deepest feelings, dreams and aspirations, and deepest sorrows, as I work on their bodies through touch. It is because I am touching them in a positive, nurturing, way. They feel they can open up and let down their guard. Also, people carry their traumas in their bodies and need to give them a voice when they are touched in a nurturing way. I often know more about them than they share with their spouses, lovers, or best friends.

> **Application: Use this understanding to increase communication with the people you care about.** Touch to connect with your deepest feelings. Make sure you know the difference between sensual/sexual touch and touch that just connects two people on a deeper level. Most often, what is needed in communication is touch that connects and expresses appreciation, or empathy.

When my daughter was young, I noticed that one of the best ways to calm her when she is angry is to gently touch her cheek or arm until she calmed down and then we could discuss her issues.

Hugging

Let's talk about hugging. The importance of nurturing touch has been seen in numerous studies on touch deprivation. *Infants will actually die from lack of touch even when their nutritional needs are met.* We have an innate need for positive nurturing touch. Our bodies respond to a hug by lowering our heart rate, and blood pressure, slowing our breathing, relaxing our muscles and boosting the function of our immune system. And just think—it's free, non-habit forming and good for you.

Some cultures touch far more than others. Studies show Americans touch one another the least on a social basis. We really are starving for nurturing touch in our world today. Let's make it a personal campaign to connect deeply, authentically, and warmly with each other in a safe way; both emotionally and physically.

Hugging is a way to connect with others and show your affection and appreciation. It can also be a great relief to re-connect after a disagreement with a hug. Researchers have shown that we need **eight hugs a day for maintenance and 12 hugs a day for growth.** WOW! How many of us really get that much positive touch?

I like to hold my arms out to the side and invite a hug by saying, "Would you like a hug? I'm a hugger." If they want a hug they will say yes. If not they can tell you honestly "Not now or no thanks." Be conscious of how hard you squeeze. It's not necessary to smash the other person. Also really make contact, a hug from the side, or with one arm is half as satisfying and beneficial as a full-on hug. Try to make yourself the level of the person you are hugging. If you're taller, then stoop down a little. I'm short so if I want a really satisfying hug I stand on the bottom stair so I'm even with my man.

Most of the highly satisfying hugs I've ever received are from friends. One friend exuberantly picks me up and twirls me around when he's really happy. I love that. Another lifts me off the ground and gives a satisfying squeeze but not too hard. He's very tall and it brings me up to his level. Another friend gives a full on "bear hug" without actually hurting and lingers long enough to add a word of encouragement or a compliment. This is highly satisfying.

Another female friend taught me that you should hug on both sides for balance. If you begin the hug with your head to the other person's left side, then finish with an embracing hug to their right side. Touch your sternums together and really let your hearts bond for a moment. This is an amazing feeling. It really is different to get hugged on both sides. It feels very balancing and very nurturing.

Sexual touch has its own appropriate arena and can bring a bond and a bliss that transcends description. *When used improperly, or forced, it can cause great immeasurable devastation.* Hugging doesn't need to have any sexual overtones and is often best when it doesn't. (It just depends upon whom you are hugging.)

> **Exercise: Start today to give and receive a minimum of three hugs. Try working up to twelve!**

Romance Your Spouse/Lover

Recently there seems to be a *revival of romance*. I love it! I think you cannot have too much romance. If you look at the amount of romance novels sold, you can get a clue as to the hunger that women have for romance. (I can proudly say that I've never read a romance novel, instead I prefer to "live my own.") Most of my life was spent in just trying to get through the day and meet my basic survival needs.

Now that I have healed, I made having fun a top value and priority in life! I make sure that no matter what else happens there is something fun and playful that I do for myself or with someone. Some might consider this hedonistic, but since my life has been filled with trauma and seriousness, I find it a delightful balance. I learned that taking time to have fun was the most needed thing in my life. I have already established deeply ingrained habits of responsibility and spirituality and I know I will not neglect these, so now I'm having FUN!

I have written "Show Me You Love Me " coupon books with creative and fun ideas for increasing romance and love between a couple. Included are many of the most enjoyable things I have done to romance my man and increase intimacy in our relationship. With 52 coupons, you can do something fun once a week for a whole year! They are available for purchase through my website at: www.mynameisphoenix.com

Some of the ideas found in them are:

- Learn to give a relaxing massage with suggestions on how to do it.

- Write a mysterious love letter using "invisible ink". You can make it really suggestive and send it to work with them.

- Exotic applications of whip cream and chocolate sauce.

- A Romantic Dinner—with a twist for the daring.

- Leading your lover to you with a trail of chocolate.

Build Loving Nurturing Relationships

I cannot estimate the full value of loving relationships with family members, spouses, and significant friends. Relationships are the bread of life to me. I would be poor indeed without the love and friendships that I enjoy.

I think that building and maintaining healthy, nurturing relationships with others is the primary task and blessing of our lives. Make it a priority in yours. When you near the end of your life, it's doubtful that you will look back and say, "I wish I had spent more time working, or reading the newspaper." The true significance of your relationships will dawn on you with clarity. Don't wait until then and have to look back with regrets. This is probably the most helpful perspective that fighting off death did for me.

A friend recently told me, when I had asked for advice in a relationship, that the way to find my own answer or "truth" was to ask myself, "If I had one week to live, what would

I regret NOT DOING in regard to that relationship?" WOW! That brought instant clarity about what I really wanted. I've been blessed when facing death to look back at my life with no regrets. I pray I will never lose the perspective of knowing what truly matters in life—people.

> **If all else were taken from me, but I still had loving relationships I would be rich with the things that matter most.**

Establish Authentic, Meaningful Friendships

Share your most authentic self with selected confidantes. The rewards of vulnerability in exposing your truest hopes, dreams, desires, struggles and faults with someone who truly validates you is PRICELESS. *The world is full of superficiality.* People are yearning for the opportunity to really connect on an emotional and spiritual level with others.

Create and reinforce genuineness and the exchange of meaningful emotions with one another. We form our deepest bonds with those that listen with empathy and keep confidences with. Also we form life-long bonds with those we share compassionate service with and for.

Self-disclosure can be frightening and leave you feeling vulnerable if it's not reciprocated. Yet the potential rewards are so great if you are selective about whom you confide in.

Overcome Superficiality in Relationships

Confidantes are like the cohesive force and structural support that holds up a magnificent work of architecture. Their importance cannot be adequately estimated. Without confidantes, (someone to really pour your heart out to, knowing that they will be gentle with it), isolation and despair can overcome your world. So often, we hear of tragic suicides when a person feels they had no one to talk to and felt no one cared. Their suicide note was the first hint of what their true feelings were.

> **I believe that if you are earnestly seeking, you will find people to connect with on a deep emotional, spiritual, and intellectual level.**

We are all seeking for acceptance and a connection to others on a deeper level than most of us engage in.

There is so much superficiality in the world. People talk about the weather and trivial things when inside they are longing to connect and share feeling, ideas, and desires. We must be the kind of person who is comfortable engaging on the deeper levels. It is risky when you share your inner self and feelings with another. If they ridicule you or betray your trust, it can be devastating. *Make sure that when you are choosing to disclose your inner self you have a "safe" audience.* Betrayed confidences can be extremely hurtful. The isolation that plagues our society and all of the despair and loneliness out there could be greatly reduced if we would quit being so superficial in our relationships. Find confidantes with whom you can share your inner thoughts and feelings.

I have heard it said that women share their problems to bond, not to resolve them. I say, stop it! If you are sharing your problems and horror stories with anyone without the intent to change it or do something about it, you are energizing those situations in your mind and body. If you talk about it continually they will continue to be a problem for you in your life. The more you rehearse, talk about, and think about them (without a resolution) the more traumatized you will become.

The brain may think that each time you talk about it, it is going to happen again, or it is currently happening. It fuels adversity to talk about it unless you also include discussion about what you did or are going to do to fix it. It's a self-destructive way to bond with someone by sharing "pity parties."

Develop Intimate Relationships with Trusted Friends

Intimacy means when you share your deepest, authentic, emotional, self—not necessarily having sex. An important component of an intimate relationship is learning how to give and receive a meaningful compliment. Seek opportunities to compliment and affirm others about their integrity and valuable characteristics, as well as their appearance, and intellect. When a compliment is given, accept it graciously with a sincere thank you—not a statement to minimize their compliment.

Seek deeply connected bonds with a few people of true integrity. It's been estimated that we need three deeply intimate relationships to have a healthy, productive, life. If you can develop more, do it! Relationships are so much more powerful and meaningful than possessions or achievements.

> **Be cautious whom you disclose your inner feelings to, but encourage it in our society.**

Cherish People Above Acquisitions!

Exercise: Who are your three most trusted confidantes?

____

____

____

____

Take the time TODAY to call them or get together with them and let them know how valuable they are to you. Never take these relationships for granted.

If you don't have three trusted confidantes, make it a top priority in your life to begin making more friends so you can find your truest and best relationships.

Exercise: Who is someone you know that you could develop a closer relationship with? Make a plan to get together today.

____

____

____

____

____

____

Where is a place you could meet someone to form a friendship with?

____

____

____

____

Think of your favorite activities, recreational pursuits, social clubs, or even church. Is there an opportunity for you to meet more like-minded people at these places or functions?

Brainstorm some new ways to make friends.

____

____

Get Out of Caustic Relationships

I respect myself enough to disconnect and release myself from abusive, toxic, or destructive relationships, even if the relationship is with a relative.

Lesson: I fully believe in the concept of turning the other cheek as advocated by Jesus. However, there are people that no matter how many times you do this, it will only escalate their abusive behavior. When a relationship is not based on mutual respect and tolerance of each other's needs and values, a closer look needs to be taken. **Sometimes regardless of how many times you acquiesce and deny your own needs and feelings just to keep the peace—only you suffer the consequences!**

Respect Your Feelings

Disregard for your own feelings and needs negatively affects your emotional and physical health.

When your needs and boundaries are constantly ignored or violated you're going to suffer. In this circumstance, I believe that you should terminate the relationship. I think it is our duty and responsibility to show people what healthy, respectful, relationships feel like by demonstrating them in our actions. **This means that when a person has directly violated your personal space, or values, you need to let them know. Hold them accountable.**

Here are examples of assertive messages you could give to someone who has violated your boundaries

- "When you tell me it makes me look fat to wear the scarf as a belt around my waist, I feel hurt. Please don't make comments about my weight. It's my own concern."

- "When you say 'Your breasts don't look so big now that you've gained all that weight' in front of my friends and family, I feel embarrassed and offended. Please just let me be concerned about my weight." If they still don't take the hint you might say, "I have asked you repeatedly not to discuss my weight, the next time it happens, I'm going to ask you to leave my home. I don't have to tolerate this from you."

Unfortunately, I actually had to make both of these assertive statements to my mother. It was one of innumerable areas where she criticized my looks, feelings, and values. The rest of the history (physical assaults) is found in a previous chapter. When I asked for her behavior to change, and stated how I felt about the constant criticism, her caustic behavior escalated exponentially. **Finally, I determined it was not worth the price I was paying emotionally to continue the relationship.**

I could have continued to "turn the other cheek and choose not to be offended" but the criticism was incessant and I didn't have the desire to continue when I knew it was only getting worse. I was receiving no benefit from the relationship. It was not remotely nurturing or loving, as I define it. I spent many years asserting my feelings to no avail, so I finally quit engaging and said "enough is enough".

I believe you should always negotiate for change and seek to establish mutually beneficial and respectful relationships. It's our duty and obligation to try to teach others what healthy interactions feel like. However, you cannot control another person's behavior and sometimes the appropriate thing is to simply end the struggle and let go of the relationship. This is especially difficult when the relationship is with a sibling, parent, lover, spouse, or significant friend.

I live by the credo that if you have respectfully requested that someone not violate your feelings, rights and values, and they continue to do it, move on. This might mean a change in employment, friendships, possibly teachers, and sometimes termination of relationships with family members. We each have the right to be treated with respect.

> **Why go through life enduring emotional pain when you have the power to change it?**

When I decided I was no longer willing to compromise my value of only participating in nurturing, mutually beneficial relationships, I was severely chastised by the people who wanted to continue the abuse and by other "churchgoers"—the ones who decided that I must not be a "True Christian". This was very hard to deal with; I felt like a "bad" person for a short time.

For a while I felt my world shrinking and fewer relationships were available to me. When I determined the pain of participating in toxic relationships was truly greater than isolation or the judgment of others, my life was flooded with like-minded, healthy, nurturing people who regularly express their love and appreciation for me. I simply had to make room for them by clearing out the negative relationships. At first while in the process of clearing, I didn't have the faith I would find better people. I just knew that I would no longer live the way I had been living.

So once again "after the trial of my faith (literally) came the blessings."

When to Terminate a Relationship

The decision to terminate a significant relationship should be the last resort and not the first.

I also think it should be a matter of prayer and meditation.

In no case should people intentionally subject themselves to a relationship where they are being physically abused. Get out! Or at least have a wise plan of escape—a stash of money, and/or a separate bank account in another bank, an extra set of car keys, a number of a safe friend and for a domestic violence hotline/shelter, a bag packed with passport/necessary papers, birth certificates, clothes for a week for you and the kids. Know that when you are ready to be free from violence, you will find supportive ways to get out. Please know that emotional abuse can inflict deep wounds that are difficult to heal. They may be even harder to heal than physical injuries. When you turn the other cheek to an abuser, you may pay with your life!

Just say no to abuse!

Releasing Yourself from Caustic Relationships Is Acceptable To God

My religious beliefs teach that God cast out one third of his spirit children from heaven in our pre-earth life. This was because they wanted to destroy the rights and agency of others to choose and they disregarded God's authority and openly rebelled against him, rejecting his laws and the plan for our mortal experience.

If God decided that some of his own children could no longer be in his presence because of their toxic behavior, (the war in heaven) I can use the same pattern in my life. It's okay for me to get toxic people out of my life.

Forgiveness:

If you have been victimized in an abusive relationship, many "spiritual/religious" people may push you to forgive! While forgiveness may be an important part in the healing process for the violated, no one has the right to tell you when that needs to be accomplished or even that you must do it at all.

Forgiveness can be the healing balm that frees the victim to move forward. If you force it prematurely, because of pressure or a feeling that "you should just get over it!" you may not have the opportunity to adequately grieve, or feel appropriate anger for the violations. Then you victimize yourself, once again, by denying your needs and feelings. If you stuff your feelings, instead of releasing, or reframing them, they will show up in physical manifestations like body pains and other health problems. The feelings must be adequately addressed and then put to rest. Otherwise, you just act on them at a different level—the body. Don't short-circuit the beauty of the grieving and healing process. If you are truly seeking to forgive, you will have the right attitude that will allow the cleansing process to be completed and then forgiveness of your abuser will heal the wounds.

Don't let someone else tell you when you have to forgive— that timing is between you and God.

> **Forgiveness comes as a part of the grief process and is most often the last step to a long and sometimes painful emotional cleansing process.**

I Used To Wonder What Was Fair About Forgiveness?

If someone violates you and destroys parts of your mind, body, and spirit, and your ability to trust; are you then required to just forget about it? It seemed horribly unfair!

As I struggled with this issue, the understanding finally came that forgiveness has nothing to do with the abuser—it is for the victim.

You know you have forgiven when there are no more thoughts about retaliation, or there is no intensity or energy left in the memory—only peace. It is a miraculous process, and it's available to anyone who seeks—it but it requires enormous effort!

You will know when you have learned this principle when you choose to forgive what seems unforgivable.

> **Forgiveness is the cleansing of the soul and the sweet peace that comes when the event or the person no longer holds any power over you.**

If you lack the ability to let go and forgive, do all that you can and surrender the rest to God and I believe you will be strengthened in your ability to forgive and heal.

Forgiveness Exercise:

I'm sure you have noticed that when you are really angry with someone you recoil at his or her touch and you avoid physical contact with them. After I had processed my anger and grief, I was ready to forgive the people that I had experienced my most traumatic experiences with.

Since I relate to others mostly through touch and talk, in my forgiveness visualization, I imagined giving them a nurturing massage and as I touched their body I would think of sending healing thoughts and energy and I would say out loud, "I forgive you." Although I never had the opportunity to actually do this, the healing that took place for me emotionally was astonishing. I felt like it was really over.

Try imagining giving a hug, kiss, or other affectionate gesture to someone who has truly offended you.

If it feels more cleansing, you could visualize doing something nice for the offender, like giving them a substantial gift, building them a lovely home, or wishing them other good things. Although they may not deserve it based on their actions, *this forgiveness visualization is for your healing!* It will make a big difference in your feelings and healing.

If you feel resistance to doing this exercise, you may need to vent your feelings of anger or sorrow first. Write a letter telling them exactly how you felt about what they did, and don't hold anything back. Don't send it! Instead burn, or tear it into little pieces and bury it. Just do something that symbolizes or makes it "over" and out of your body.

Use music therapy or get a somatic emotional release massage. When the feelings are truly diffused you are ready for the next step of forgiveness.

Additionally, I wrote a letter to each of them, stating, "I forgive you for....", and listed each offense until it had no more energy behind it. It was not intended to be sent, it was simply for my own healing.

To finalize this new feeling of forgiving and letting go, I wrote a message on my mirror with eye pencil, (you could use a dry erase pen) "I forgive ________. (Add their name) I am fearless and free!"

Each time I see these people or think of them; I rehearse in my mind, "I forgive them—it's over!"--This way my mind remembers my new feelings instead of recycling the old hurt and anger.

Now you try it. Pick several of these exercises and do them. This may take some time. Give yourself permission to work on them as long as you need to. If anger resurfaces it's not an indication that you have not forgiven as much as an indicator that you still have more hurt inside to heal. Do a few more of the above suggestions to release the hurt, then the anger, and eventually the forgiveness will surface.

Best Behavior is for Family

The greatest opportunities to learn and express selfless love are found in the home. It is here that we feel we can truly be ourselves. We can take off the many "hats" we wear in our different roles in our employment, school and with acquaintances and be our truest self.

What a tragedy that some people use the home to be their worst self, venting their anger and frustrations on their loved ones instead of dealing with them appropriately.

> **Your actions in the home are the truest measure of your integrity and character.**

> **Application: Remember to appropriately touch and express affection to your family.** Openly express verbal and physical affection for each other. We do this by giving each other hand & foot rubs, massages, and lots of hugs and kisses. We tell each other how much we love each person frequently. As a parent, I write letters of love and encouragement to my children. I print them on special paper and put them in a personal binder for each child and enclose the letter with a plastic cover to preserve it. I also started writing love letters in a special journal for each child and one for my partner.

When conflict arises, ask yourself:

- What is my part in this problem?

- Do I understand the other person's point of view?

- Is the preservation of a loving relationship more important than the issue at hand?

Since loving relationships are my top priority, I can effectively deal with problems when I remember that the relationship is of primary importance, and the conflict is of secondary importance.

- **If viewed from an "eternal perspective" or substitute "long-term perspective," how important is the situation I am dealing with now?** This means I believe earth is only a temporary place where we are interacting now, and that our relationships can transcend this earthly sphere.

- Are we placing correct priorities on the most important things, or do we busy ourselves with trivialities and entertainment that alienates us from our loved ones and squanders our time? Do we devote our time to the things that matter most?

- "In this family we talk out our problems because we love each other!" This is a common affirmation for us. Teach mediation and problem solving as a way of life. You must address and acknowledge the *feelings* of the person you are having a conflict with first, or an acceptable solution is highly unlikely. Remember, take care of emotions first, and then move to conflict resolution.

Parenting

I cherish my children and love them beyond my ability to express because of the extreme sacrifices I made with my mind and body to get them here. I want to give them all I can to prepare them for a rewarding life, not free from difficulty, but with the ability to meet any challenge with faith and dignity. I am now rewarded by watching them parent their own children with love, while teaching them accountability.

Transcend How You Were Parented

It is our obligation as parents to transcend whatever parenting we received and improve upon it! There is always room for improvement. Stop making excuses. Stop reacting from old habits and strive to improve yourself and pass it on to the next generation. Re-examine cultural parenting patterns and do what is best for your children, not just what was always done before.

> **The most important contribution I can make in this life is to teach parents to be more loving, to teach children (mine or someone else's) how to solve problems effectively, how to think for themselves; and how to engage in nurturing, respectful, loving relationships. In essence, to teach them how to live with integrity.**

Children are the ones who can carry the message to the next generation. I cannot afford to neglect this. I can work to enlighten, and empower my peers, which is very important, but I believe that if I can help to educate children so that they don't have to work so hard to undo habits of thought and action, I have truly made a crucial difference. I hope that this will ring true with you also.

> **Children are an heritage from the Lord. --Psalms 127**

I have never talked "baby talk" to my children. Consequently, they had a great vocabulary and an ability to articulate their feelings and thoughts at an early age. I observed that they could understand concepts that are complex if explained to them in words they understand. I often had adults comment on the maturity of my children in their relations with others. I believe it is because I never "talked down" to them.

> **Application: Listen to your children with empathy and the intent to understand more than just the words they are saying. Learn the strengths and relating style of your family members.**

Show children respect by giving them your full attention when they are talking to you. If we want to remain close to our children, we have to be available when they are ready to talk to us. If you absolutely can't talk to them at that moment, tell them "I can't talk to you right now but what you have to say is really important. I will be able to talk with you at such and such a time." You may need to get an idea of the topic so you can remind them later. Then make sure you follow up or it will be perceived as one more broken promise. So often, if you just take a minute or two to listen, they can tell you what they need to and because you dropped what you were doing to listen, it builds trust, rapport, and love. It tells them, "You are important to me, and I care about what you think and feel".

People, not things or money, bring us the ultimate happiness in our lives. Show them with your eye contact, empathetic listening, and help them name their feelings, or just validate their feelings. This illustrates to them that they are very important to you.

Application:

Never tell a child, "don't" or "no" without an explanation of why. It will build animosity if you tell them what to do without giving them an understanding of what your reasons are. Say, "Don't play near the road, *because* you may be hit by a car and hurt or killed." It makes more sense to the child. We all appreciate being given reasons for the expectations others have of us. If there are reasons given it helps a child to learn about the process of reasoning and consequences.

Demanding strict obedience without reasons can be perceived as threatening to the child's autonomy and builds resistance and often rebellion. The old phrase, "Do it because I said so!" is insulting, and will turn on you as the child increases in their need for autonomy. When you give the child a reason for your request or rule, they are much more likely to obey and it teaches them to reason. Suddenly, they realize there is logic in what you are saying.

Speak at the level of the child's understanding. Treat the child respectfully since we all appreciate that. Once when my daughter was young and demanding, "Why should I?" in an angry, defiant tone, I simply said, "Do I ever talk to you that way?" I waited for an answer, then she sheepishly said "No." I replied "Then don't talk to me in that tone of voice."

Next, I explained why I had made the request and she obeyed my request. I would never have been able to request and get that respectful tone from her if I didn't show her by example what I wanted in the first place. I try, in all of my interactions, to treat my children as though their feelings and needs are as important as my own, because they are to them. (I'm equally confident that there are some areas that I could have improved upon as a parent.)

Application:

When raising my children and they wanted something from me I asked myself, "Is there any reasonable way to do what they are asking of me while not denying my own needs and values?" (This is valid for any significant relationship.) In essence, I treat my children almost as peers, but I make sure that they understand that although they have a chance to make a request and give input into what happens in our relationships, since I have more experience, I will make the final decision about what happens.

I use logical and natural consequences as discipline instead of any form of "punishment" whenever possible.

Punishment will only invite anger, rebellion, and emotional distancing if used to be the ultimate authority. Using domination, control, and manipulation to rule in your home will ultimately fail.

If you talk it out, without shouting, and listen to the child's point of view before passing judgment, you may learn something! You may even change your approach or solution to the problem.

I have found that when I lower my voice and speak with absolute determination people know I mean business. It is far more effective that shouting!

Remember that no one, especially children, likes to be dismissed, invalidated or ignored. We all have a need to be heard and validated.

Cherish Children

- Teach the next generation to love more, think more positively, and have more people skills than you!

- Break the chains of dysfunctional family relationships.

- Be honest with your feelings. Children know what you're feeling and often what you're thinking. Validate their perceptiveness by naming your real feelings. It helps them learn about feelings and how to deal effectively with them.

- Treat them with the respect you would give to a cherished friend.

- Try to understand their feelings and perspective before making a judgment or enforcing a consequence.

- Touch them with nurturing intent. When my daughter was young, I tried gently stroking her cheek, while she was vehemently explaining her side of an argument with her brother. After evaluating the situation, I concluded that she had yelled and hurt her brother while he was trying to walk away from a conflict. I touched her in a nurturing way, and sent "love-beams" through my heart and hands, and I spoke with a soft voice. As I explained my expectations of her, she softened her voice and her attitude and her posture. Soon she was apologizing and ended the evening by giving all of us a foot massage. I went out of my way to praise her for her affection and kinder attitude. The touch connection is so vital. I am sending a message of love and acceptance just by touching.

- Have you ever noticed when you're angry with someone you don't want to touch them? We often avoid the act that would bridge the misunderstanding and heal the hurts more quickly than words alone.

- Take time to kick up your heels and play like a child with them. Ask them, *"Can you come and play with me?"* Make a special date time just for them.

- Get to know your child as an individual. What are their strengths, interests, talents, fears, and ways of learning and expressing love and receiving love. Do they learn and relate to the world by feel (kinesthetic), visually or through hearing?

- Do you know what your children think of you? Ask them how you are doing as a parent and friend.

- Teach them problem solving and conflict resolution by your actions. **Of all the things we teach our children whether intentionally or not, mostly they learn and repeat how we problem solve and how we act when we are angry.** Let's teach them life-skills about how to empower themselves through problem-solving and effective negotiations.

- **Engage them in problem solving as a way of life**. Take the opportunity to point out when you are experiencing difficulty or challenges, and tell them how you handled it.

- Help them evaluate the effectiveness of your solution. Teach them to be expert problem solvers. Teach them that they can tackle any problem and give them opportunities to test their wings.

- While they were growing up, I selectively involved my children in conflict resolution. If they see two adults modeling negotiation in a loving, respectful way they will be so far ahead in their own relationships. Think of how hard it is to overcome dysfunctional ways of problem solving.

- *Give your children and the world a gift—teach them how to resolve conflict with love.*

Exercise: Do you know the way your child relates to the world and feels loved? Take the time to analyze if they relate to the world predominantly with touch, with words, or with actions. Do a specific loving act in their way of feeling loved this week. Record your results.

Life Purpose: Figure Out Why You're On The Planet
Finish What You Came Here For!

I strongly believe we are not taken in death until our mission or life purpose is complete! That is to say, if we are actively working to accomplish all we can for good and seeking to fulfill our "divine calling", we will not be taken prematurely. If we are not living with integrity, I don't believe we are worthy of divine intervention.

> **The more we are open to receiving help and changing ourselves, the more assistance and knowledge we receive about what our life's mission is and how to complete it.**

I believe we agreed to experience certain lessons in life before we came to earth. It is not the same as pre-destiny in which we have no control over what happens, but it is an acceptance of certain experiences or criteria available for our greatest growth. I believe we will experience what we agreed to experience in our pre-earth life. However, it is our choice what we do with it. We can refuse to learn the lesson to our detriment, or we can make the experience or lesson work to our benefit and highest good.

> **When you are trying to seek out and complete your purpose in life, you will be protected and aided in doing so. Some people appear to be taken in death prematurely. That may not be the case. It may be our lack of understanding for God's time frame that causes us to perceive the death as premature.**

The "Jonah Principle"

Whether you believe this story to be real or simply a powerful metaphor, it has application to each of our lives.

Lesson: Jonah was called to preach repentance to the people of Nineveh. He had already tried to get them to listen and but they wanted to kill him instead of repenting, so he ran away from God's "mission" for him. He tried to hide on a boat, but as turbulent seas were battering the boat around, Jonah recognized that he was the reason for the roaring seas. The Lord was trying to get his attention.

Jonah told the people to throw him overboard and save their own lives. A huge fish then swallowed him. He was kept alive in the belly of the fish without being digested for three days. During this time Jonah decided that he would fulfill his mission and return and preach repentance to the people of Nineveh. To his amazement many of the people did repent and the Lord spared them from the destruction He had promised if they did not repent.

As soon as Jonah repented and accepted his mission, he was spit out of the belly of the fish. The Lord protected him from the wrath of the people of Nineveh and his life was spared. In addition, he was the means of sparing many other people's lives because of his obedience in calling them to repentance.

We all came to earth for a purpose. Our challenge is to find what it is! I believe that God, a loving Eternal Father, sent us to earth with a game plan. I believe that we agreed to basics of the game plan and accepted it. Many of our life's problems are exactly tailored to teach us the lessons needed to accomplish our mission or life purpose.

If you examine your life, and the problems that repeat themselves, you will find a clue to your greatest potential growth and life purpose. My life purpose is different than yours. We are always given divine assistance in achieving our life purpose if we are sincerely seeking it and are humble enough to accept the way in which the lessons are taught.

We Come to Earth to Learn Some Specific Lessons

> **Our circumstances will bring those lessons to us in a variety of forms. We can learn quickly and move on, or move slowly and suffer, but the lesson will be repeated until we learn it!**

We are not responsible for other people's actions. They have their agency to act out good or evil; however, we can sometimes attract or repel those people and circumstances by our thoughts, beliefs, and actions. Some people call this "magnetism" or the law of attraction.

We have complete responsibility and choice in how we think about events and how we react to them based on the information we have at the time.

I strongly disagree with the notion that we are where we are in life exclusively because that is where our thoughts have placed us. I have heard it said that if our circumstances are less than what we think we want that there is an underlying belief system or subconscious desire that puts us where we are. *I believe there are other purposes and factors for where we are.*

For example, look at Jenny's life. Beginning in early childhood, she was constantly in situations where she was victimized. There was a continuous stream of people in her life who recognized her submissiveness and capitalized on it for their own gratification. Did she come to earth to be victimized because she liked it or was comfortable with it? Did her thoughts originally place her in the ideal circumstance to live out a life of perpetual victimization because she did not have positive thoughts as an infant? Absolutely not!

Jenny's Lesson: "To stop being so passive, I had to look for new ways of thinking and relating. It wasn't easy but it is definitely worth learning. I was born with a burning desire to be independent and to stand up and fight boldly against the plagues of our society like violence, emotional and physical abuse, and misuse of authority. I was blessed with an understanding of my personal worth, which kept me moving in a direction that ultimately became my freedom.

Initially, as hard as I tried, I could not break free from victimization because I didn't have the information I needed to change. As I matured and public awareness was turned to the issues of abuse in all its forms and the unimaginable devastation perpetrated through violence, resources became available to learn a way out and I did!"

> **We are where we are because it is the ideal starting point for our growth. We stay where we are only if we do not learn to change our thoughts, habits and gain mastery over ourselves.**

Leadership

Make a Difference in Someone Else's Life

Author's Experience: I had the great privilege of meeting a friend that touched my life and heart in a way that no one else could have. He was uniquely qualified for the job. We spent many hours sharing our thoughts and the deepest feelings of our heart about our lives, and our challenges. He was a dreamer, very lyrical and articulate. He loved books and on his meager wages would buy me his favorites. I was surprised to discover a man with such passion for life, and who loved to talk and tell stories. This man told me of his family and his desires to improve his life, make a great life for himself, and bring his family to the "land of opportunity." He worked with his hands as a roofer. He related to the world through his exquisite verbal skills, quick wit, and with his body through hard physical labor and a love for dancing. I was amazed to find a man with such similar feelings and interests as mine.

He taught me to see myself through the eyes of someone else, whose vision was a little clearer than mine at that time. I was struggling with my self-identity and feelings of worthlessness because of the toxic relationship I was involved in. He helped me see how wrong these feelings were. He inspired me to have a new sense of myself and of my worth. **One day he said to me, "I have traveled around the world and I know many people. You are the most kind, good, beautiful woman I have ever known."**

This meant the world to me because I admired him and felt he was qualified to give that opinion and it was said with the deepest of sincerity. He was a gentleman with impeccable manners, and he never tried to make the relationship into anything that would violate my standards. He touched my soul! He reflected back to me the kindness and compassion I showed to him. He gave me the courage to look at myself in a different way, which was the catalyst for the tremendous changes that have taken place since then. **Without his influence, I might not be who I am today. He left a long and lasting memory and changed my life forever.**

My experience with Holly: After the experience of having someone else help me see who I really am inside, I began doing that for others. A close friend, Holly was struggling under the burden of low self-esteem and debilitating back pain that did not respond well to surgery and kept her in such pain for so many years that she sometimes contemplated ending her life to get out of the pain and despair. *She said that whenever life overwhelmed her she thought about suicide.* She had many layers of emotional and physical pain. As she lived in another state, I kept in contact with her over the telephone. Because I had known her for many years, I could remember what she was like before the accident that was a precursor for her pain. I knew of her desires and interests and I could see her inner and outer beauty, which she had forgotten about herself.

> **I firmly believe that our greatest problems are the gate to our greatest victory.**

I started by asking her about all the reasons that she had to want to be alive. I think that you have to start with the core, which is a will and desire to live. It's where I had to start when I beat death. I had to wake up each morning and rejoice that I was awake and alive! I had to see the joy in each moment and be glad for it.

> **You learn to be grateful for things you never considered very significant when you are near death**

As we reminisced about the better days and the hope of a better future, her attitude began to change. I challenged her to pray for the strength and desire to live and overcome. I tried to encourage her to evaluate her reasons to live.

She took the challenge, and began re-evaluating her life. I reflected back to her all of the abilities and talents that I knew she had and told her what having her in my life meant to me. *We all need to know that we are needed.*

When I was very ill, I could not muster the desire to live for myself. I had to ask myself who needs me? My children needed me and it was the only motivation strong enough to keep me fighting through the rigors of disease and death, over and over. As I shared this insight with her, she began to understand that her family needed her and depended on her. But for her that wasn't as strong a motivation as she needed.

Each of us has a life that is totally unique and we have things to offer family and friends that no one else can. We have to figure out what we have to offer others and be willing to share. Holly understood this principle because her desire to help others has always been one of her greatest qualities. I have often said that she is the most selfless, caring friend I have. I count myself very blessed to have her in my life. The key for her motivation to live was that I told her if I could come from "mostly dead" to where I am now, she could too! She believed me. I told her how much better her life could be if she would just trust that all things work together for our good. She started to see things from a different perspective, which helped to improve her emotional outlook.

> **We each gain insights from our problems that may be crucial for someone else to learn from us.**

I noticed when she was in severe pain, she sounded like my young children in her responses, and her expression of the way she felt and saw her life. I told her that I had observed this pattern and wanted to approach our interactions from a different angle. I let her know that she could let me know if anything I said offended her. I was concerned that the switch from treating her as a peer, who wanted to vent and express herself, to a sort of a child figure, might bother her. She just seemed like she needed some mothering. Because we have always been very frank with one another explaining this approach worked well.

Since I have studied parenting extensively, I began to treat her like I treated my children when they had a problem. I started reflecting back to her what she was saying, what I understood her feelings to be, and asking her what options she thought she had to change the situations, instead of just listening and empathizing. I had always thought of her as a very mature person but when she was in severe pain, which was a lot of the time, she reverted to childlike thinking.

She didn't know she had any options or personal power to work her problems out.

Lesson: I began urging her to take responsibility for her own thoughts and actions. I challenged the way she perceived many of the things in her life and asked her to use the technique I stumbled onto, which is turning a situation around and looking at it from the opposite side of the spectrum. I asked her how that might change the way she thought or felt about the situation.

I used the same firm, loving tone of voice I use with my children and she began responding in an astounding way. She started seeing outside her paradigm. She began to start thinking of other options she had not considered before. She began reasoning for herself because I was expressing my confidence in her ability to figure things out. When she got stuck with something, I would make suggestions by giving examples of how I had worked through a similar issue. I saw her start to mature in an accelerated way. I had always been perplexed at why she couldn't reason when she was hurting or overwhelmed because she was so capable in most ways. *I just had to meet her at the level she was at when she was in pain.*

Although I never felt suicide was a good option to get out of my difficulties, I did feel like giving up sometimes, and just give in to the effects of my terminal illness and die. I had a limited perspective of how she felt. I just listened to her express her pain and uncertainties; I knew that there must be some incredible trauma locked in her body because she was not responding to conventional treatments. (This is a frequent scenario with the clients who come to me for bodywork. They have tried about everything else and I'm the last stop before they do something drastic.)

Holly had the chance to come and visit me for short visits every few years. During these visits, we did extensive bodywork for releasing trauma and cellular memories. She began to release many layers of memories embedded in her body. They were a huge factor in her pain. As we began to release and reframe them, she began to have less pain and a different posture and tone of voice. The despair was gone from her voice. I heard an optimism that I had never before heard. She began to make other changes and her life is transforming on many levels to one that is pleasing and rewarding most of the time. **Most importantly, she has quit wanting to kill herself!** I don't take credit for this. I'm just the facilitator, but if she could do it without my input, she would have a long time ago. **She just needed some new information and someone who believed in her ability to get through her private hell.** I will expound on some of the things released during her bodywork in the chapter on healing bodywork. It was profoundly moving to be a part of that experience of healing for her.

> **Whenever we discussed a trauma or difficulty, I insisted on ending it with a solution or a game plan for how to solve it. Then it was not left hanging—as though it still had energy or power over anyone.**

Another thing that I did to help her out was to refuse to dwell on the negative. I sent her my list of personal affirmations and code of conduct that I had come up with to turn my life around. She liked them and started using them. Eventually she began making her own affirmations and recently completed her own Code of Conduct Statement. She called me and excitedly told me how differently people were reacting to her now. **I affirmed that once you define yourself in writing, people will begin treating you that way. It's quite miraculous!**

I let go of my need to "make her see the light" and she began to fill in the void. I continued to affirm to her that she could and must take control of her life through her thoughts and actions. I was amazed at how she responded. She still needs validation like we all do, but now our conversations are uplifting and exciting as we cheer each other on to the next triumph.

Author's Experience: A man I know is totally immersed in genealogy. He was telling me how awed he was to understand that he was related to famous people (kings of a foreign country generations back) who had great strength and character. I replied, "Why not become that kind of person yourself? Make yourself into the kind of man that your posterity will look back at in awe." He seemed shocked. I told him it was my objective in life to create a legacy that touched the lives of my family and friends forever. I have noticed that the only place I find parallels to the magnitude and amount of trials I have faced in my life are in the Bible—like Job. Another man was listening and then he paid me the highest sincere compliment. He said "You could stand toe to toe, as a peer, with any great person in history." I was highly honored to realize that he acknowledged this about me. It made me realize how far I have come in my healing journey.

> **Be the kind of person your posterity will look back on with awe and honor, one who forever touches the life of someone else for good.**

> **Application:** I have volunteered in my church, and the schools my children attended, and I make myself available to share the knowledge I have gained with individuals who really want to change.

Find your niche in charitable work or uplifting mankind. Then spend some of your time and resources to benefit that cause. You will be amazed at what it does for you.

Take the time to be a blessing in the lives of those closest to you. Listen with empathy and elevate the relationships you engage in.

When you find your life purpose share your vision with others. Live to make a difference in the world; on a personal and if possible a national or global level.

Devote Yourself to a Cause Greater than Yourself

My children were the impetus for my exhausting fight against death. When I felt like giving in to my disease and just wanted to go home to God; where there was no more pain, or suffering, they would say or do something that gave me strength beyond my own.

One day when I felt quite overwhelmed and was crying in my room, my son then about three years old, came into my room and asked why I was crying. I told him I was very sad. He dropped to his knees and uttered a prayer that was incredibly powerful and sincere, asking God to help his mommy get well and be happy. Of course, I was crying even harder then because I realized his enormous love for me and that he truly understood my needs.

His faith was that his prayers would be answered and I would be comforted, and I was. I realized then that my presence made a difference to someone. I was getting through to my children. They needed me and my influence could help them. So often, I had felt that my life meant nothing to anyone but me. At that moment I knew it meant something to others!

> **Application: Find the thing in your life that evokes such passion and devotion that you want to devote yourself to doing it a majority of the time.** Find your "calling in life" and then pursue it with zeal!
>
> Maybe that calling is to be a fantastic parent or spouse, maybe it is volunteer work at your favorite charity, or perhaps it's finding the cure to a devastating disease. Whatever it is find it and do it!

I believe my life purpose is to help others heal, feel joy, and reach their potential

Psychic/Emotional Debt

When we help someone with compassionate service, whether that comes in the form of emotional, financial or physical assistance it creates a "debt" in the mind of the giver and receiver.

It's very important in healthy relationships to keep the scales balanced. Fredric Lehrman in his audio program "Prosperity Consciousness", advocates letting people, even friends, pay you for your help, services etc. This can come in the form of actual repayment in money or in a returned service the receiver then gives back to the giver.

This is a really important concept. When one gives and never receives back you can feel used or worn down. When one receives and never gives back you can feel guilty or like a "charity case" which can make one feel put down or inferior. Let us all help each other by giving and receiving. If you can't give back to the giver, then "Pay it Forward", like in the movie, and give to someone else because you have received.

Uncommon Avenues to Healing

Music Therapy & Emotion

Don't let emotions such as anger and sorrow stay in your body! They can cause dysfunction and disease. They can lead to the destruction of your health and relationships.

Anger in-and-of-itself is not "bad" it can be a strong stimulus for action and change, but if it's not diffused to release the energy it can lead to violence and destruction. Anger is often a secondary emotion to the primary emotion of hurt.

Sorrow by itself can be healing, cleansing, and there is Godly purpose in sorrow for sin. If you don't express it and let it out, it can lead to regret, unwillingness to forgive yourself or others, and an inability to recognize and feel the blessings and good things in your life. It can lead you to shut off your heart and emotions.

Sometimes in order to not feel sorrow or emotional pain we shut ourselves off from our feelings. This is essentially "living death." We cannot be fully alive without feeling deeply. Find outlets to release and diffuse the emotions that feel stuck and have a negative influence on your happiness or effectiveness. One of the most effective ways I know of to release emotion stems from my deep love of music. I studied voice and music performance as my major in college.

When I feel frustrated, angry, or even felt like I want to fight, I listen to some passionate stirring music to get the emotions out. I can vicariously release my anger, rage or sorrow through the sounds of the music or singing along with the music.

I love to dance so I often move to the music as well. Sometimes I choose music with specific lyrics to address the situation like when I wanted to get over a bad breakup. If I needed to cry I would listen, and sing and cry. I might play the song repeatedly until the feelings were spent.

> **Application: Some of the most effective music for releasing anger is considered "classical."**

(Strictly speaking the classical era was from 1725-1800 AD however, most people call this type of music "classical".) I recommend this type of music because it cuts right to the core of emotion. You don't have to think about lyrics that may not apply to your situation. Lyrics can sometimes be a distraction. Make sure you don't play music with violent lyrics or something that incites you to anger. **The idea is to diffuse it and replace the anger with peaceful calm feelings.**

I find the music of many Russian composers very passionate and useful for dispelling anger and frustration. I like Igor Stravinsky's "Rite of Spring", and "The Firebird Suite"— of course it's about a Phoenix. I also like Hector Berlioz, "Fantastic Symphony", and Bela Bartok's "Sonata for Two Pianos and Percussion". Some of Richard Wagner's music is very stirring as well. There is such emotion and passion in their music, I relate to it on a cellular level. The feel of it stirs my soul—and cries out for freedom. It ignites my passion, and releases anger, and frustration. After listening to some "angry music" to diffuse the emotion, I replace the intense feelings with something mellow and harmonious. Any of Mozart's music works well to soothe the savage beast, but some of my favorites are "Flute Concerto in D Major" with flute, harp and orchestra, and "Concerto for Clarinet and Orchestra in A". I love the symphonic poems "The Moldau" (Vlatava) by Bedrich (Friedrich) Smetana, and "Prelude to The Afternoon of a Faun" by Claude Debussy.

Releasing the emotion through music keeps me whole and healthy. Get some classical music for your emotional health.

Sometimes I need good old Rock and Roll. The lyrics take me back to my youth or have lyrics that resonate with how I'm feeling. It helps to get out the feelings I'm seeking to diffuse.

Be aware of the effect that lyrics have on your psyche. When words are accompanied by music they are sometimes convey very strongly into our minds and we remember them for years. For example how many little advertising jingles could you sing, even after years of not hearing them, if I gave you the name of a product? Be aware of the messages you are feeding your brain. They have a strong effect on our emotions and well-being.

Karaoke:

Maybe you just need to gather some friends and go belt out some songs together.

> **Application: Give your emotions a " voice"—name out loud what you're feeling and affirm that now that you have recognized it, and voiced it, it is over and done.**

There were many years in my life that I felt "I had no voice". No one cared to hear how I felt and no one wanted to change his or her behavior to stop the enormous hurt I had inside. No matter what I voiced, it did nothing to change the circumstances. **Eventually this feeling translated into an actual loss of my singing voice, my outlet for my emotions, and my way of singing praise and thankfulness as well.** As a voice major, I had extensive training in how to use my voice to project the sound to fill a room without amplification. I had a three-octave range and a lot of power. Because of my feelings of helplessness at not being heard, I lost my singing voice for five years. It was like tearing out my heart. I remember saying out loud, "God take my life, but don't take my voice." I had largely defined who I am by my ability to sing. I had some soul searching to do. I had to find out who I really was. I had to realize the source of the loss of my voice. Then I had to change my circumstances by giving myself a voice.

After I started to voice my protests, set appropriate boundaries and stand up for myself, I began to have hope that I would someday regain the beauty of my singing voice. It took tremendous personal change and years of work but I did eventually regain my voice. I am still working at regaining the flexibility I once had but I have regained three full octaves.

Healing Bodywork

It's been said that hair stylists, bartenders, and massage therapists hear more intimate details about people's lives than most others. I believe this is because people drink to drown their sorrows and then tell strangers what might be best kept to themselves. Hair stylists and massage therapists are touching people and because of their close proximity, their clients often share details that they don't tell to others. Hearing these heart-rending stories was a factor in leading me to a style of massage/bodywork that is specifically designed to release trauma from the body and mind.

Because I always have a nurturing intent as a bodyworker, I'm often told things that clients don't even tell their spouses or anyone else. This is especially true when I am doing bodywork designed to release emotional and physical trauma. It has been a tremendous help in my life and for many others for whom I have done this type of bodywork. In this chapter, I will elaborate more on this kind of bodywork, and tell you how you can find someone to do this kind of work for you.

Author: One thing I have found to be unequivocally true is that the body doesn't lie! I'm aware of the concern about "false memories" that can be suggested or even intentionally programmed into the "memory" of an individual without their awareness. I believe that this could happen under certain circumstances. I do not believe that unreal or imagined events can become so real to the individual that they also affect the body in the dramatic ways that I have seen people react, and have experienced myself, with the release of trauma during somatic emotional release bodywork.

The mind may be tricked, deceived, or programmed, but the reality is locked into the tissues. When I am working on someone and their body is "unwinding" by moving through the movements of being raped, assaulted, or they are heaving repeatedly as though they were vomiting, it is not a false memory! Nor was it a minor event in their lives. I have worked with individuals who have released memories of sexual assault and brutality almost beyond comprehension. Their emotional responses along with their body's response are so powerful that I simply don't believe it is possible to make up or have a false memory of these events.

The proof is in the body. An individual could come up with an elaborate story of trauma but if it is not consistent with the body's response, it may well be a false memory. However, real trauma is often so horrifying that they often can't actually verbalize a lot of details, but their body is highly reactive and shows evidence of serious trauma.

Additionally, an event may affect individuals in different ways. One person may survive a brutal assault and function fairly normally without the symptoms of major trauma. Another individual who was threatened with rape or "only" fondled may react with severe symptoms of trauma. It varies greatly.

The point is, no one else gets to determine whether you are justified in your feelings or reactions to something that was traumatic to you. Just acknowledge your pain and trauma and get it out of your body so that you don't have to continue reacting to it with present day symptoms of past events.

If left unresolved, (meaning changing it into a positive mental, emotional or physical outcome) it is left in our bodies, to produce the stimulus for continued negative thoughts and experiences. This truth is something too crucial to ignore. You can't afford to walk around with traumatic "cellular memories." The consequences are too great.

Author's Experience: So how can you fully and finally resolve any negative or traumatic experience? The most effective way I have found is through bodywork. It has had a greater positive impact in relieving the pain of my past than any other factor. I want you to know what it is and how you can get it for yourself. It may be the most important thing you do in overcoming adversity and giving your body the vital energy, it's capable of having!

Some of the most dynamic healing that can occur happens when you access trauma at the level where it is stored in the body. This fascinating field of study and bodywork has become my passion! I have been able to do the most effective work of relaxing and healing the body at a cellular level. I was lead to this type of bodywork when my search to unload some of the trauma of my life had not proven effective through traditional counseling.

Some of my life's experiences had touched me so traumatically that the terror was locked into my body. Regardless of how much I wanted to unload the feelings I had about them, I could not get them out of my body. When talking with various counselors, one of two things would invariably happen. **I would either "dissociate" from the memories and be able to discuss it logically and unemotionally; as though it had happened to someone else, OR I would feel as though I was re-living it completely!** My whole body would shake, I'd feel nauseated, get very cold all over, and my diaphragm would tremble. That's how my body experiences terror. It became so upsetting to actually talk about the things I wanted to get rid of, that I felt like I was being re-traumatized with each counseling session. I determined there must be a way to release this horror and I was going to find it! I did.

I was lead to a workshop directed by Peter Levine a psychotherapist and bodyworker. Then I took bodywork training sessions from others like Clyde Ford, and Charles Daily who were also finding very effective ways to treat cellular memory (traumatic experiences that cause memories and emotions to be trapped in the tissue of the body).

Here is my interpretation of this kind of bodywork and why it's so effective.

The phenomenon of people storing trauma in their bodies and having the trauma triggered with the full intensity of emotion, experienced at the time, was most noticeable in post-traumatic stress disorder (PTSD) victims of wars and other monumental tragedies. It was as if they were re-experiencing the trauma repeatedly without a resolution of the experience. People began researching and studying why and how this happened.

Massage therapists and other professionals noticed it wasn't just isolated to experiences of severe trauma and that in fact all of us have some experiences that were too difficult for us to fully process at the time of the event. Consequently, these memories were stored in the body for further resolution. The trauma or insult to the body can be emotional, physical or chemical in nature, and each of us carries a backlog of unresolved experiences waiting to be released and "re-framed."

If you have a pleasant experience or conversation with someone, it is stored in the normal way in the subconscious mind but not necessarily in the cells of the muscles or organs. However, if we have an experience that causes fear, sorrow, anxiety, anger, pain, severe distress or illness, the body stores this memory completely intact for the individual to process or "reframe" at another time in the body. If a person does not have enough information to process the experience; perhaps they are too young to understand, too badly injured or in severe shock, then the body keeps this experience "alive" in a sense. The body reacts to it daily.

These memories seem to have more power because of their negativity and unfinished characteristics. They can exert power over how we react in many other situations and experiences. This can cause the body to become worn down and develop diseases. It can leave us feeling that we don't have the emotional energy or capacity to deal with present day stresses. It can keep us re-living the experiences in our dream states.

Overall, these traumatic events keep us from fully functioning and being alive to our fullest capacity until they are released.

Without resolution, our bodies become overwhelmed with these memories causing pain, restricted movement, and chronic tension called "armoring." These unresolved memories influence our posture, health, and decisions—even our personality. Once enough information is received or correct stimulus is applied, the body can "reframe" the context and content of the traumatic memory and free us from re-experiencing the trauma repeatedly.

Charles Daily, the developer of Holographic Memory Release, compares these cellular memories to an answering machine that stores every experience we've ever had in the form of a message. The traumatic messages that have not been successfully resolved or reframed are played repeatedly. It's as if every time you want to listen to a new message you have received, you have to play back through years of old messages to get to the current one. Eventually you run out of space to store new messages on. Additionally these traumatic memories are stored much like a "holographic image" with all of the details of the original experience.

There is some debate as to where these "cellular memories" or "somatic" (meaning body) memories are actually stored. Is it exclusively in the brain, where past research suggested all memory is stored, or are these traumatic memories stored both in the mind and the body? My opinion, based on several decades of using this type of bodywork to relieve the traumatic experiences of my client's, leads me to the conclusion it is stored both in the tissues of the body and in the mind. It appears that these memories are stored in the muscles and connective tissue themselves along with information in the brain. I compare it to a lock and key. The muscles, tendons, and ligaments hold the memory and are the "key." The brain stores a portion of the memory and I compare this to the "lock." In order for the memory to be released and resolved both the brain and body must be involved.

One style of bodywork I have used with tremendous success is a technique I developed based on information from several different styles of bodywork and philosophies in releasing somatic memories. I call it Interactive Trauma Release. (Somatic memories are traumatic memories and emotions trapped in the body.) I attended a workshop for Massage Therapists in the early 1990's by Peter Levine, author of: <u>Waking the Tiger, Healing Trauma: The Innate Capacity to Transform Overwhelming Experiences.</u> Here is my interpretation of the information he presented at that time.

Levine suggested that you need two of three elements to be present in order for trauma to be released from the body or re-framed. These elements are emotion, a physical feeling or sensation, and memory of the event. If you can connect two of these three you can have resolution.

Several of the participants had some trauma of their own that he facilitated their resolution. One woman had been in a severe car accident. She had nagging pain after that (a physical sensation). Levine asked permission to touch her shoulders and then asked her to close her eyes and see if she could remember any more details of the accident (which connected her to the memory of the event) or if she could get in touch with any emotions about the experience. She remembered a number of details that she had forgotten on a conscious level, which lead her to experience pain sensations in other areas of her body involved in the accident. As each of these places was touched or addressed, she then was able to connect the memory to the sensation. Finally, Peter facilitated a guided imagery visualization that although it was not exactly how the event actually ended it gave her mind a "mythical" but much more satisfactory ending to the trauma. It was fascinating. She felt much better afterward.

Author's Experience: I had a dramatic experience at the workshop. I am very private about the most severe traumatic experiences of my life. I had absolutely no intention of sharing with a large group of strangers the most horrific events of my life, but I could not seem to help myself. As I disclosed what had been some of the most horrifying events of my life, including the time someone tried to murder me, I kept covering my mouth because it felt as if I was compelled to speak, but I didn't want to. I was afraid my experience would not be believed or that people would be uncomfortable with me afterwards, and I just didn't want to take this risk.

Often when someone unloads their deepest secrets, people just don't want to know. Fortunately, I was very supported by other bodyworkers. Peter helped me out, not by touching me, but by taking me through a guided-imagery visualization. I was already experiencing the emotions of extreme agitation and fear. He mirrored them back to me and asked a few more questions about the experience to help me reframe it. I was clearly aware of all of the details of the memory, so I had two of the crucial elements. I just needed to reframe it. He asked me what I would have done if I could change the experience and have a different ending, or what my body felt like doing at that moment.

Frankly, I felt like bolting. I wanted to run away before I exposed any more vulnerability or said anything else. He had me close my eyes and run as hard and fast as I could imagine in my mind until I felt safe. In my mind, I ran from hell I had experienced. I visualized running for miles until I felt some peace starting to settle in my body. Then in my mind, I concluded by resting on a large rock near a stream listening to the pleasant sound that soothed my mind and body.

Now, that is not how it really ended, but it gave my mind a different way of looking at the experience. In reality I could not fight or effectively flee, but I was given this outlet through creative visualization and re-framing which released the trauma from my body.

I left the seminar and had some intense reactions in my body that night and the next morning. I experienced what can be called a "healing crisis" as more layers of trauma continued to exit my body. I vomited profusely and became so dizzy that I could not drive myself to the workshop the next day. I had to get a ride. I was determined to go because I felt despite the reactions I was having that I was going to experience some significant relief. I told him what had happened to me when I went home and he explained what was happening.

Occasionally in some types of healing, like this kind of bodywork, someone who has experienced extreme terror might have vomiting and dizziness as their body cleanses itself emotionally and physically. Once I learned that this was part of what my body needed to do to heal, I was relieved. The nausea and vomiting stopped and gradually the dizziness left. *I have not had any of my clients have this type of intense reaction.* I have had some that experienced the sensations of old injuries or a release of emotions in connection with the bodywork as the body finally lets go of the trauma.

It's such a relief to know that it's over! One of my male clients had an intense cold reaction for several days in his body after a massage. We had released the trauma of an assault that broke many of his facial bones and required reconstructive surgery.

Lesson: Research in the field of psychology has shown that if an experience is too traumatic for the person to deal with or understand, the brain "walls off" this memory as a means to protect the individual and allow them to function at some level. In a sense, all memory of the actual event can be blocked from the conscious mind, although it is present fully intact in the subconscious mind and in the tissues of the body that participated in the event.

Obviously, this is not an ideal way to live but it preserves the individual until they have the necessary skills or understanding to begin working through the trauma. This memory can be repressed for many years or indefinitely. However, it does affect the individual. They may have unexplainable feelings, anxiety, panic attacks, and a myriad of health problems, but cannot relate it to a particular experience in their conscious mind. **It is not uncommon for a victim of child sexual assault to block this memory until they reach their thirties or forties.**

We All Have Some Form of Trauma

Each of us has experiences in our life that cannot be fully processed at the time of their occurrence.

Jenny's Story: An overview of my childhood

"I grew up in a home with unspeakable violence and abuse. My parents presented a respectable image, participated in the predominant religion of the areas where we lived and created a facade that allowed them to commit acts of abuse upon their children and others that are unimaginable to most people. They were part of a community organization that were very loyal to each other and patronized each other's businesses as well as supporting each other in criminal activities that were very effectively hidden from mainstream society.

One has to actually experience this kind of abuse to believe it exists and even then you don't really want to believe it, it's simply too painful to truly acknowledge the reality of it for a time.

My mind and body are a "walking witness" against my parents and their associates. There is virtually no part of my body unaffected by this terrible abuse. When I was two, I chose to defy their nefarious practices. I was determined that although I could not prevent what they did to my body, I would not let them manipulate and control my mind. I paid for my rebellion in my flesh. To date, I have had two hernia surgeries in my childhood and, as an adult, I've had my uterus, bladder and nasal cavity reconstructed. These surgeries were all needed to repair the damage done to my body from the hideous abuse done by my parent that was part of my childhood.

"Because of the damage to my body and my quest to conquer the abuse—to fully reclaim my mind and body—I was led to bodywork to release the trauma. I have greatly benefited from bodywork designed to release trauma locked in the body. When I receive bodywork/massage in a safe, protected environment the terrifying experiences are often relived in dramatic, full detail as if they were still happening, but the beauty is they are then finally released!

As I acknowledge the experiences, and reframe them by examining them and then reassuring myself that they are not happening anymore, I can resolve the trauma, reclaim my body and triumph over abuse. It has been a long journey that continues. I am amazed at my body's resilience and my own indomitable will as I recover from these experiences.

"These early experiences shaped my choices and my experiences as I attracted many more abusive people and traumatic experiences into my life. It has been a huge struggle to change these patterns and begin to attract and participate in healthy interactions with people. A huge part of my success has been because of my participation in Martial Arts. I can now use my body in ways that sets very clear boundaries for anyone with malevolent intent. It is tremendously empowering to know that I get to choose what happens to my body now (at least in most situations).

Bodywork to release trauma has been the single most helpful factor in my healing process."

The most exciting news is that cellular memories can be resolved and the trauma is finally over!

If you have had good experiences with a caring psychotherapist or counselor, I'm very happy for you--stay with it. Very likely, this type of bodywork is something your counselor has heard of and would be supportive of you receiving it. It can be a powerful adjunct to the work you do in counseling.

If you haven't been able to fully resolve your difficult life experiences through counseling here is my explanation for why this happens. Some of us have elaborate sabotage mechanisms built into (or intentionally placed) in our subconscious mind. No matter how willing our conscious mind is to overcome and heal, the subconscious mind is acting out another agenda. This can make traditional counseling alone ineffective. We want to get over something and try to talk it out, but in our gut or body, it's really never over. Our bodies keep reminding us of the experience through pain and dysfunction, fear or anxiety and even illness.

I believe the reason talking alone is often ineffective is we cannot isolate an experience and break it down into the components that allow full resolution by left brain, logical, discussion of the trauma. Sometimes the trauma is so great that the memory is not accessible to our conscious mind, much less our speech. Sometime the trauma happened before we could talk and although we were pre-verbal, the terror is still there but you cannot give it a voice since you had no words with which to understand the experience.

Our entire bodies are sensory organs and participated in these events. It's impossible to fully express the intensity of some experiences through speech alone. It does not resolve the trauma. Resolution requires the full participation of our being. *Fully participating means accessing the body parts that were involved in the experiences, along with the feelings or emotions felt at the time of the trauma; and possibly those feelings occurring afterward, and the accompanying memory itself—which may or may not be accessible through speech.*

It's not always necessary for the memory to come to the conscious mind to be resolved. It depends on the style of bodywork used to release these cellular memories. **It is clear however, that it requires a hands-on approach to coax the body into yielding up its secrets and freeing the mind and body from the trauma. A licensed professional, who specializes in somatic emotional release or cellular memory work, can very effectively address these memories through hands-on bodywork.**

It's not necessary to re-experience the trauma to resolve it with somatic emotional release bodywork. It's possible to give the mind and body an affirmation before beginning the bodywork session. For example, if something is too difficult to remember on a conscious level, the body and mind can still release it by connecting a physical sensation—like a sore neck or a headache—with an emotion experienced when that area is touched.

Additionally, about 90% of the women who come to me for this style of bodywork have sexual assault issues. Obviously, I don't re-traumatize them by insisting on touching the areas involved. The body can very effectively release the trauma from the pelvis through touching the sacrum (the triangle shaped bone at the bottom of the spine) or by gently laying a hand on the abdomen. These sites can release issues of rape and childbirth.

You Can Handle What Comes Up!

A client won't have a memory or emotion come up that they are not ready to process.

The body and mind will protect the memories until the person has the ability to resolve it. If they have anxiety about this fact, I have them repeat the affirmation

"I don't have to remember what happened, I can just connect to a physical sensation, and an emotion and then the memory is released." Giving the mind these instructions can facilitate tremendous breakthrough in healing.

See Me for Individual Bodywork Sessions to Release Past Traumas

I consider this kind of bodywork my life work.

My "Interactive Trauma Release" Technique: This is the technique that I developed by putting together several others isolated techniques from various bodywork styles.

Here's a little background about how it evolved. I explain to my client that we are working together to connect an emotion with a physical sensation, or a memory. This I learned from Peter Levine. It makes so much sense based on the way our bodies' process and store information, and how my own body would not release the trauma without all these elements present together.

I make sure that whatever I do, I ask permission to touch them, let them know exactly where I'll be touching them and ask them to tell me when they're ready for me to begin. Of course, I never touch the genitals. This empowers and informs my clients. This is something that Clyde Ford, a Chiropractor and Bodyworker, explained is very important to do with victims of sexual assault. I usually start with the element of physical sensation since most people are somewhat aware of areas of pain or discomfort in their body. I gently place a hand on the area of pain or discomfort with about the same pressure exerted by the weight of a quarter on the skin. When I do this, their body will begin to move in response to my light touch. I learned this technique from Cranio-Sacral work from the John Upledger Foundation. My hand will follow the movement of their tissue. This has been referred to as "unwinding".

The idea is that the tissue involved will repeat the same pattern of movement it experienced during the initial injury or trauma. In Cranio-Sacral work, you guide the tissue into a different movement if it stays stuck in a repeating pattern. This technique was applied only to several specific areas of the connective tissue that run in a horizontal plane. I reasoned that any area must be able to respond and unwind with the correct stimulus. As I began using this unwinding technique on other areas of the body that were experiencing restriction and pain, astounding releases occurred and the tissue freed itself and let go of the spasm.

I continued practicing this technique with great success along with traditional Swedish and deep tissue styles of bodywork. I decided to marry this unwinding technique with the somatic memory ideas presented by Peter Levine. Very exciting things began to happen.

My mind was opened up to information about my clients that I could feed back to them to assist in releasing their trauma. I was guided to various areas of the body that seemed completely unrelated, but were somehow connected in the clients body because of simultaneous injury in both areas; or because that's where that individual stored their sorrow or anger or disappointment. Initially, I relied heavily on them to supply the information about emotion or where they were hurting, and where I should place my hands next.

Very soon, this became a completely intuitive process for me as a facilitator. I knew just where to touch first on the body and where to touch next. I had information enter my mind; like flashes of pictures or events that were not part of my own experiences, or a feeling would suddenly engulf me.

At first I found this quite odd, then when I started being brave enough to tell them what I was "seeing" behind my closed eyes or "feeling." They would excitedly tell me that was part of their experience or memory, or that it was the same feeling that they were having at the time. Occasionally, the feeling wasn't exactly the same one they were feeling but it was closely related or varied in intensity. For instance, I might say, "I'm picking up a feeling of anger," and they would say, "No, I feel rage!" Sometimes I'll say, "I'm picking up a lot of confusion," and they'll say "I am confused" but as soon as they voice confusion, the clarity of an emotion or memory will enter their mind. It is extremely helpful to have this intuition or insight when working with a sexual assault victim because they are frequently dissociated from the sensations of their body and their emotions as a means of coping. When I can mirror what I'm picking up off from their body, it suddenly clicks and becomes clear to them. They often insist on telling me what they're remembering or feeling. I never make it a condition of the treatment to share with me what they're feeling or experiencing, but they can simply say, "I've connected with a feeling or a memory, together with the physical sensation of where your hand is resting on an area of discomfort."

I think this ability to sense and feed back their experiences and feelings is an intuitive gift that seems to only operate for me when I have the intent to facilitate healing, have my hands on their body, and I let go of all the thoughts in my own mind.

I also think that this can be developed by anyone. This is why I think so. I attended a very interesting seminar by Clyde Ford a chiropractor and bodyworker at a massage therapy convention. It was right after the Rodney King beating and everyone was thinking about it at some level.

As a black man, Clyde was especially weighed down by the events that were being shown repeatedly on the news. It was as if we all had various intensities of grieving going on. Clyde broke slightly from what he was going to present and took us through an exercise that I'll never forget. He had us close our eyes and "embody" anger. When we had a clear sense of anger we could open our eyes and look around the room. It was amazing the change of posture present in the individuals of the room. Next, he asked us to embody several other emotions, one by one and then open our eyes to observe others and ourselves.

It was so dramatic to see the immediate changes in the bodies and countenances of the people as they shifted while they "embodied" each emotion. I think that this information is broadcast from our bodies as we have embodied the emotions elicited by traumatic experiences. By tuning in to their broadcast signal, I can feed back to them what emotion I'm feeling projected from their body. I also often see pictures of what happened to them in my mind.

One client came to me because she could not swallow her food well. It was getting stuck in her throat and it was very tight and uncomfortable. As we explored the origin of the pain she explained that her ex-husband tried to choke her to death. She said "He's in prison with Charley Manson." She explained that he was being released soon and had promised to come back and "finish the job" and kill her. She had a lot of trauma to unload! We worked together to unwind and release her throat and within about 20 minutes she was able to swallow without pain and felt much better.

As I continued working with her I kept "seeing" in my mind her body and especially her head being forcibly banged into a wall. The image was very persistent so I said, "I keep getting this image of you being banged into a wall, has that ever happened?" She was not thinking of those incidents at the time and was experiencing a block where nothing was coming up. Apparently, I got the image first because she said, "Yes, I have been thrown against a wall several times. Once I was on a cruise ship and a man was trying to rape me. I wouldn't cooperate and so he threw me against the wall. Luckily a crew member walked by and saw what was happening and I was able to escape." As soon as she said it the tissue in the back of her neck where I was touching relaxed dramatically. She could even feel the shift. It released the trauma. She was blocked from it consciously but it was being broadcast to me quite clearly. As soon as I voiced it she filled in the details of the experience and it was resolved or reframed which caused an immediate relaxation in her chronically tight neck muscles. This was the memory that was keeping the back of her neck rigid. When all the memories were released she felt totally better.

It's not necessary for someone to have this kind of intuition to effectively give a somatic emotional release treatment. However, it can be a tremendous benefit if you can find someone who does work intuitively. I have been able to teach others how to work on me. Since I'm very aware of my feelings and the sensations in my body, I can direct them where to put their hands first and then next. For me, I nearly always connect all three elements. I have an area that is hurting or dysfunctional and when I get a caring person to facilitate me, I connect the physical sensation with strong emotions. I frequently have memories come in detailed floods of information like a movie playing behind my eyes.

Holly, who I have worked with extensively using this technique never sees pictures but does connect pain in her body with emotion and then it's resolved. Occasionally, she has a specific memory come up but not one after the other like I do. Either way works. She has experienced some incredible breakthroughs in this type of bodywork.

Here are some other experiences that my clients have had with somatic emotional release treatments from me.

One of my frequent male clients came for a typical massage that included work on his back, neck, and arms. It was the first time I'd worked on his face. This facial massage caused him to be cold for days. He called me and asked if I could figure out why he was having such an unusual reaction. He said he just could not get warm. I explained it could be a memory surfacing or the body trying to resolve something.

When I get very cold after bodywork or counseling, it's because I'm processing fear or terror. I told him to come in if it didn't stop after this explanation of a possible cause. He then remembered and told me about being assaulted so severely it caused his skull to fracture and required reconstruction of his skull around his eye. After connecting with this memory and relating it with cold sensation, it was reframed and resolved. He felt much better afterward. In fact, he came back for more work of this type specifically for head, skull, and face.

His body was so ready to unload that trauma that all it took was the stimulus of having his face massaged to trigger it. If he hadn't called, I could not have given him the missing information about its possible emotional connection (that led him to recall the assault) and relieved the trauma for him.

Another male client came when I first started using somatic emotional release. He hurt first in his low back, then knees, then groin. He began laughing as the pain traveled from place to place. I asked him what was so funny and he remembered having a bat thrown by a fellow player in a baseball game that hit him in the groin and caused him to drop to his knees creating pain in his knees, low back and groin simultaneously. He had completely forgotten the incident and it was finally all connected during this treatment—which oddly made him chuckle. Of course, I had him touch the place on his groin that hurt, and when he did, the memory came up for him.

After the connection of the memory was made, his chronic low back pain was greatly relieved. He had multiple low back injuries, which I had been treating him for with a prescription for massage, but only when we connected everything did he start to make real progress.

How I give an Interactive Trauma Release Treatment

When I work on a client, I have a clear intent to facilitate the release of trauma for them. I have to let go of any expectations for the sessions and clear my mind to be a feedback monitor for them. I usually close my eyes to block out any distractions and have the client really tune in to their thoughts, body, and emotions. This style requires active participation from the person to keep their mind clear and just go with the flow of whatever comes in to their minds.

Most often, I ask them where they are hurting or feel an area that just doesn't feel right. Next, I ask them to go deep inside their mind/body and wait for an emotional feeling or memories to enter their mind. Sometime this is hard for them to do. They have been in the practice of blocking this information out for so long. I have been blessed with a very clear intuitive sense that is very active when I'm doing this kind of bodywork.

Sometimes, I'll have glimpses of events or emotions enter my mind, which are not my own experiences. If the person is really stuck and can't come up with anything on their own, while I rest my hand on the area of pain or dysfunction, I may feed back to them the feelings I'm picking up off their body. Occasionally, I will feed back an image that comes to my mind.

Holographic Memory Release (HMR) is another style of bodywork designed to release trauma and cellular memory. You can do an internet search to find HMR practitioners. The Holographic Memory Release Technique is quite different than the one I developed but I have used it with great results for myself and my family and clients. It is a technique that does not require any active participation from the individual receiving the treatment. The developer, Charles Daily, feels the less information you give them about what they might experience, the more freedom their mind and body have to reframe whatever is needed during that session.

HMR releases are very light contacts made on the spine, and sometimes the pelvis. The client is fully clothed and can even go to sleep during a session if that's how their body responds. It is totally unnecessary to connect with any memory or emotion as this is can all be done on a subconscious level, beneath the conscious awareness of the client. It is a very gentle, non-invasive technique. Because of this, the client can feel completely safe and it provides an environment where traumatic memories can very effectively be reframed. Most often HMR is done in a group setting with several clients receiving a treatment in the same session. It can add to the healing experience exponentially to have many people experiencing healing relief at once. After a gentle contact is made by the practitioner on a client's body, the client is allowed a few moments to assimilate the stimulus and reframe whatever the body has chosen to work on in that session. As the layers of "armor"—chronic tension and holding postures are released from the body, new freedom of movement and thought can be experienced and dramatic healing can take place.

I have found this technique incredibly helpful and effective. Although it varies widely from other styles of somatic emotional bodywork, the body readily responds to the gentle touch and stimulus provided to release trauma from the body. I used this style exclusively on my children when they were young for somatic emotional release. I wanted them to grow up without all the excess baggage so many adults carry around. I get this type of bodywork on me when I have a specific memory I want to work out, or if I'm aware of dysfunction or pain in a particular part of my body that I want to specifically address. *I use HMR for any type of suppressed memories, or anytime I don't want to be actively involved in the process and I just want my body to figure out what it needs most for that session.*

Trauma Anniversaries

Without resolution, cellular memories and trauma can be recycled on an incredibly accurate time schedule over and over.

I had a client who was uncharacteristically intense and angry during the month of December, consistently. He also has some subconscious stimulus that causes low back injury in May. He has injured himself just by bending over twice, on the exact same day in May. At first he was reluctant to accept the fact that there was something unusual going on when I suggested he might be experiencing the results of a cyclical cellular memory. After the second back injury on the same day exactly one year apart, he started paying attention. I suggested that we do some somatic memory release work for him. Some amazing things came up for him that he had not connected to his current low back pain.

During one treatment with somatic bodywork, I was working to release his sacrum and the memory of a car accident that occurred many years ago came up. He had never consciously connected with the low back pain caused in that accident since the pain in his neck from the whiplash injury overpowered the pain in his low back. Yet there it was, still waiting for him to acknowledge it and resolve it. As the memory unfolded he was aware of getting out of the car and feeling very shaky and weak (from shock) and recalled having an immediate intense pain in his low back as soon as he stood up, that was quickly overpowered by neck pain. He had forgotten the low back pain because it was blocked by neck pain.

Another memory waiting to be reframed was a groin injury that caused intense pain that had occurred many years before in a Judo class. As we worked on various areas of his body, memories of longing and disappointment over his first love came up for reframing. This memory was 25 years old yet still had an influence on the feelings and postures in his body.

As we began the treatment, I asked him to clear his mind and think of what difficulty or trauma he experienced in December that was influencing his current behavior. He had been unable to figure out why he was feeling and acting in such a hostile way so I suggested it might not have anything to do with the current circumstances and to look back to uncover its origin.

In just a few minutes, he remembered that he had received a layoff notice from a company that he had saved several million dollars for by the work he had done for them. He had been employed with them for many years. It would have left him without a job in December. The layoff actually occurred several months after December, but he had been strung along for several months in a very unpleasant situation before his job was terminated. He felt very hostile at the time about the way it had been handled. This unresolved trauma had such a hold over him that it recycled hostility beyond his awareness of its origin every December.

He was very happy to get to the bottom of this. After he connected to the memory and let it go in the session he had an immediate improvement in his behavior and attitude.

His bodywork session strongly illustrates the point that unresolved trauma is never really over until it is addressed. Everyone has some kind of cellular memories that are keeping them from fully functioning until they are reframed, and the best way to do it is connecting with them with this kind of bodywork. They may be memories from as far back as your birth. For example, even a very old injury can be a factor in the severity of pain experienced in any additional injuries, because the first pain to the body was never fully resolved. It creates layers of unresolved tension, and pain at the site of the injury and the memory storage site. So often, it cannot be resolved because in other types of treatments the elements of emotion, memory, and physical stimulus—or pain, are not released simultaneously. Both the car accident and the groin injury were causing some type of holding pattern, or stimulus for re-injury, because they had not been satisfactorily resolved at the time of their occurrence.

This type of cyclical cellular memory has been a strong negative influence on my health and my feelings. Fortunately, I learned how to resolve them when something comes up for me. It is something I work to release regularly since I have had many traumatic experiences in my life and have many layers of pain and memories needing reframing. For instance, October used to be a month of deep sorrow, loneliness, and melancholy feelings. I finally connected to some memories that explained these feelings for me and helped to resolve them. It seemed as though they had been with me forever and each year seemed to produce a few more negative experiences in October. One of the memories was the murder of my sister's friend that I mentioned in the chapter on intuition. It was a bizarre and deeply sorrowful experience to be forewarned in such an unexplainable way. It was only one of many disturbing experiences in October.

When I taught someone how to do this work for me, I started to get some dramatic relief. I have had a similar problem with the month of February. It's been a month of excruciating pain that recycles over and over. I have had five miscarriages and ten kidney stones in the month of February over the years. I had to be hospitalized during my only successful pregnancy for complications with severe gestational diabetes in February.

I am writing most of this book in February as part of my cleansing and healing process. I am also making sure that I get some good bodywork to avert any potential problems. When I have unexplainable feelings, emotions, or pain, I get some bodywork done immediately and get it out of my body.

One of my friends experienced unexplainable deep sorrow, and anxiety, for an unknown reason on a certain day of the month. As she searched her mind, she finally realized her father had died on exactly that day four months previous. She came for some bodywork on the anniversary of his death to help to reframe that trauma so it would not be a continually negative memory. We also made sure to do something very lighthearted and happy things on that day to replace the old feelings of grief and shock.

> **Application: It is really important for us to replace memories of old pain with new ones of joy. Holding onto the difficulty and negativity of the past helps no one.**

During some of many bodywork sessions for Holly, she recovered some deeply disturbing memories. Some were available to her conscious mind, and other had not been for many years. As I helped her to reframe her experiences of sexual assault, I guided her through some visualizations that allowed her to imagine fleeing the situation and create a different visual image for her mind to hold onto. It greatly relieved her distress about the situation and was a catalyst for some very positive healing. She also recovered a memory of being taken as a very young child and having a plaster of Paris cast put on her face by a sculptor so he could have her image.

It was so traumatic for Holly to have her face, eyes, mouth, and nose covered for an extensive period of time with plaster, that she was certain she was going to die. There were straws inserted in her nose to breathe. I had to actively keep affirming that she was safe and she could now let this go because she had remembered it. In addition, the man molested her while she was in this helpless situation.

We were able to confirm with her mother that this was an actual event! It was so terrifying she had blocked it from her mind until her adulthood and only released as I worked on her face in a somatic emotional release session—*four decades later*. Most of her childhood, until the age of eight or nine, has been totally blocked from her memory.

As we continually worked through these repressed memories of childhood, Holly has connected to lost parts of her past and is finally able to begin healing the pain. She is doing much better now. She is one who may not have survived without this type of bodywork, as she had strong desires to end her life because of debilitating chronic back pain and emotional suffering.

"Connecting the dots" for her in bodywork sessions has yielded some explanations for this pain and has allowed her to reduce her pain levels significantly. It is a continuing process for her, as it is for many. As long as we're alive we will have experiences that may need to be reframed but they will be fewer, and our coping mechanisms will increase dramatically, if we can let go of the old trauma through bodywork.

In the workshop by Peter Levine, he related a story of a female client who kept having auto accidents because of her history with an abusive father. She was a victim of long-term incest. Her only appropriate nurturing experience with her father that made her feel nurtured, came after a severe auto accident. Her father who usually only abused her, held her tenderly and nurtured her while they waited for emergency help.

This tenderness was such a powerful experience for her that she found ways to recreate auto accidents—many of them, to re-experience the feelings of the only time she felt being appropriately loved and cared for by her father. This was all created on a subconscious basis until Peter began asking questions that "connected the dots" for her and brought this pattern to her awareness. After she realized what was happening, she was able to break the cycle through Peter's bodywork and professional counseling.

Application: Find someone with specific somatic/emotional bodywork experience to work on you to release your cellular memories. Find a professional bodyworker who specializes in HMR or somatic emotional release and get some treatments. It may be the most important step in overcoming your trials that you can make!

I find that many areas of my body have issues that need to be resolved, often simultaneously. Since I can't figure them all out at once, it works best for me to get someone else to work on me. **Since I recognize that not everyone will readily find a professional who specializes in this type of bodywork, here is a self-help technique you can use until you find someone to work on you.** Don't give up. It's worth going to another state to get this kind of work done. The healing can be phenomenal.

Application: Self-Help Technique:

If you can't find someone you trust to do this work, here is an alternative method that may help. When you are experiencing an emotion, or area of pain or dysfunction in your body that does not seem to be linked to a current event or condition, you can ask your mind/body aloud what the emotion or memory is aloud.

By listening to your thoughts and body you can usually come up with an answer of what it is about. If there is no clear answer, you can place your palm over your forehead to help your mind access a memory, or remember an emotion. Alternately, you can place your hand on the sore or dysfunctional body part and pose the questions "What is this pain or illness about?" "What do I need to do to fix it or resolve it?" Frequently, you will come up with a solution using this simple technique.

This technique works well if you are really tuned into your body. If you don't have success with this, keep searching until you find a trusted professional bodyworker to get somatic emotional release done for you.

Try touching the part of your body that hurts and talk to it aloud with your positive affirmations. Or try gently resting your hand on an area of illness or dysfunction and let your mind freely bring up whatever thought, memory, or emotion it can. This can help release the trauma for you.

Make it a habit to create *happy* memories on significant dates of past disappointment, injury, or trauma—like divorce dates, death dates, injury dates, etc. It does not dishonor anyone to do this. The dead would want you to go on living a happy and productive life. If the deceased, or a former spouse, are not the kind of people who would want you to be happy despite their absence, question why you are mourning over their loss!

Some of the possible benefits from Somatic Emotional Release Bodywork are:

- Relief from chronic pain and tension in the back and neck.

- Increased energy.

- Resolution of previously unresolved emotional and physical pain.

- A feeling of optimism and enthusiasm for life.

- Improved self-esteem.

- Improved relationships and communication.

- Improvement in chronic health problems.

- Better productive and creativity.

- Greater understanding of self and personal motivations.

- There are many other positive possibilities!

No results or healing is guaranteed. Your results may vary since each person's body responds uniquely.

Get Personal Empowerment Guidance from Phoenix

If you have been searching for a way to overcome your past limitations, you have just found it. I am a Personal Empowerment Guide and I have been a Licensed Massage Therapist since 1989. Some counselor's experience consists of only reading about abnormal psychology from a college textbook, and they have little experience with real life trauma. In addition to my education, I have lived through surreal adversity.

My life has been filled with experiences that could either make or break me. I had to learn to overcome difficulty and adversity. Like the Phoenix, I want to be more than just a survivor.

I have made it my life's quest to continually learn and grow toward my highest potential and life purpose, and to embrace the power of self-mastery. I have purposefully designed the woman I have become. I feel called to share what I have learned and help those who can benefit from my life's lessons, especially those learned through trauma.

My life's path has led me to research numerous avenues for healing and self-mastery. Many resources in this book are uncommon and unfamiliar to most people. My education and training offers me a distinct advantage to help you find just the right combination of resources to support you on your journey toward personal empowerment, and success.

When you decide to take charge of your life, you will succeed. In this book, I share my lessons learned, and the wisdom of the great men and women whose contributions have shaped my life along the way. Together we can find your path of joy and success!

For over 30 years, I have studied peak performance and personal development materials gleaning the latest resources in human potential. I have thoroughly researched and applied techniques in the areas of conflict resolution, boundary setting, personal assertiveness and trauma resolution. I have especially focused on the relationship between our emotions and physical disease, illness and pain.

Combining bodywork (massage) with the techniques of visualizations, emotional re-framing, goal setting, affirmations, and personal empowerment coaching you have powerful tools to overcome limitations and clear out the debris of past experiences that are holding you back.

You can experience an amazing transformation. You can begin living the life you want.

After reading this book you can experience Personal Empowerment Coaching to apply the principles you have read about. Your progress will be directly related to your willingness to take responsibility for your life and apply principles of healing and empowerment found in this book and through Personal Empowerment Coaching.

What to expect from Personal Empowerment Coaching with Phoenix:

I use various techniques to help you in the areas you need to explore and resolve to achieve your personal desires. Some of these include:

- **Bodywork**: As a Licensed Massage therapist, I implement several styles for Somatic Emotional Release that are designed to release and resolve trauma and dissociated memories or feelings that may be contributing to poor health, negative emotional states, or sabotaging your success.

- **Creative Visualization**: Designed to establish a pathway to your subconscious mind which will enable you to most effectively implement your conscious objectives.

- **Emotional Reframing**: Is a way to change the FEELINGS you have that are undermining your health, or goals. *Scripting* is a powerful tool you can use when you identify a feeling that is holding you back. Using this tool, you can change that feeling explicitly into what you want to feel, moving you forward rapidly.

- **Exploration**: We can work together to explore what your dominant purpose in life is. What are you uniquely qualified to do that will contribute joy to your life and add value to world at large? What do you most want most to have, be and do? We will then create your plan for achievement that you can implement.

- **Principles of Empowerment**: We live in a universe of principles that govern our life whether we understand them or not. Our frustrations are usually a result of ignorance to the principles. We can explore your role in the principles of, attraction, learning valuable lessons in adversity, prosperity, consciousness and getting in touch with the super conscious universal mind or your intuition. You will be taught the principles of the ages that enable you to truly succeed.

- **Trauma Resolution**: As long as you are burdened by negative emotions and suffering from past experiences, you cannot move into your bliss or "the zone" where you see all of life's experiences as designed to lead you to opportunities for growth and development and you live with joyful empowerment. Together we can clear out the issues that may be holding you back.

- **Uncommon Avenues to Healing**: Light sound machine, aromatherapy, and dream journaling, vision boards as well as other avenues may be explored.

- **Progress Papers**: You will be given written materials to read and exercises to explore that will guide you along your path.

Get started today with finding your bliss and living the life of your dreams.

Contact me at: MyNameIsPhoenix2@yahoo.com www.MyNameIsPhoenix.com

DreamWork and Lucid Dreaming

Author's Experience: For most of my life including my childhood, I have had recurring nightmares. I would often wake up with my sheets and pajamas soaked in sweat from the trauma these nightmares caused. I went to my endocrinologist to see if there was any other explanation for these night sweats. There was no imbalance found to create this particular symptom. Needless to say, I was tired all the time and felt anxious; even afraid to go to sleep at times, because I knew what terrors awaited me in my sleep.

The most frequently recurring theme was of being raped, murdered, and dismembered. I would wake up with my heart pounding so hard I thought I was having a heart attack. It frequently caused chest pain in addition to profuse sweating.

Lesson: When I learned a few techniques for changing the content of my dreams I was finally able to rest peacefully. I learned a technique called lucid dreaming from an audio tape designed to teach Lucid Dreaming techniques by Frank D. Young called "Relax into Lucid Dreaming". I learned that I could actually manipulate the content of my dreams and interact with the symbols and characters.

Lucid Dreaming work was the beginning of life altering success. I also learned a lot more about the possible symbolism of the figures in my dreams. I practiced lucid dreaming with some success, but before I finally gained control over the nightmares, I had to use another technique.

The real breakthrough came when I began saying dream affirmations to myself just before falling asleep. I came up with these affirmations based on what I *wanted* from my dreams, not on what had actually been happening all my life. You will find them in Appendix D: Goals & Affirmations.

> **Application: Whether you have persistent nightmares or simply want to access your dreams and subconscious mind as a place to play out your newly developing positive life, dream affirmations can help you!**

Lesson: Now when my brain is trying to resolve or reframe a past experience, I do it in my dreams. Frequently the reframing process that occurs with bodywork continues in my dreams for full resolution.

I now have found dreaming to be a rich playground for my subconscious mind to work out problems creatively and offer solutions to the problems and difficulties I am experiencing in my life. You can too!

Most of my dreams can be remembered when I first wake up. I make sure to take note of their content and possible meaning. Sometimes I even write them down to analyze later.

Keep an audio recorder or notepad by your bed to right down your dreams, their symbols and possible resolution.

My experience: Drastic changes started occurring in my dreams after using a few dream affirmations immediately before going to sleep. Many recurring dreams began to surface for resolution. I began to have familiar recurring nightmares. This time the outcome was totally different than it always was before. **The difference was that I affirmed that I was now in control of my dreams.** I'll give examples of them in the following paragraphs.

Here's a dream that came up for resolution after doing the dream affirmations before going to sleep. It's a nightmare that has repeated itself for most of my life. It is always some variation of me running away from something or someone. I am always going to be raped, stabbed, or maimed in some way. Often I know I will be killed. In this dream, I was being chased by someone who was about to overtake me right in front of my church. I think to myself, "I can't believe I am going to be raped and stabbed in front of my church." Then I realized that I don't have to run! The affirmation that "I am always safe" kicks in. I turn to my attacker and roar like a huge beast, and then suddenly I am aware that I am incredibly powerful—and safe. My attacker flees from me! Defeating my attacker had never happened before in a dream! It was a huge change.

When I woke up from this dream I realized I had finally hit on whatever key unlocked the resolution of these nightmares! The affirmations had begun working and dynamic changes started taking place.

Another old recurring dream from my childhood came up for resolution. Interestingly my mind finally understood its meaning because I had programmed it to do so by saying, "All the symbols in my dreams are easily understandable."

It is a terrifying dream that repeated itself since my early childhood. I'm riding in a car with my family up a very steep mountain. The incline becomes progressively steeper until the car loses traction and we all fall, crashing to the bottom. Sometimes when I had this dream in the past, **I would die from the crash in my dream**. (I actually fell out of bed onto the hardwood floor while having this dream once when I was twelve years old. That blows the theory if you fall out of bed while your dreaming that you're dying you will actually die!)

This time I resolved the dream while I was lucid dreaming, in a semi-conscious state, rather than an actual dream state. I used creative visualization to resolve it. As the dream surfaces, I take control. With my creative imagery, I start the ascent up the steep hill but this time I am driving the vehicle and my children are in the car. I understand that part of the steepness of the ascent was my perception of how hard it was to get there, based on old information, so I changed it in my mind to be a longer but less steep incline.

We all make it to our destination WITHOUT ANY HARM OR PROBLEM WHATSOEVER!

Finally, after so many years I intuitively knew the meaning of that dream because it used to end with all of us crashing. (This is because I had told myself that I would know the symbolism.) **One meaning is that it was a premonition to an actual event of being in a car that was going up a steep hill and rolled with me in it.**

Here is the spiritual meaning that came to me and my interpretation and resolution of the dream. I am trying to reach God or salvation with my family of origin in the car. It becomes progressively difficult to get to the destination. It is clear that not all of us can go there together because the vehicle cannot support all of us, or does not have the power to get us all there. We start to slide backward and the car tips over and we will all perish.

I understand now that I knew as a child that I needed to make my own way—even then. I couldn't rely on anyone else's actions (driving) or the people traveling with me, to get me to salvation. The reality of this did not strike me until much later in my adult life at about 33 years old.

Soon another recurring dream surfaced for resolution. The reality of this dream did not strike me until much later in my adult life. It always starts the same. I am going to a new school. (My parents moved me a lot.) It is finals week and I can't remember where my locker is, nor can I remember the combination to my locker. I know I am going to be tested, but I can't get to the answers in the books to study. It creates terrible inner trauma because I have always been obsessive about getting perfect grades.

Now with my creative imagery in a lucid dreaming semi-conscious state, I call forth my sentinel (a guardian and protector) to help me. He escorts me to my locker and gives me a piece of paper with the combination on it. The locker opens up to a vault with thousands of books. I enter and begin studying many of the books. I am also visited by the authors and receive personal instruction from them while inside this special room. When I am satisfied with my reading and learning and without any angst, hard study, or effort, I step out of the vault. To my surprise instead of being a student, I am now the teacher and I enter a room with many students who are eager to learn what I have learned.

I feel that this new outcome is what I am now living. My lessons learned through great struggle are now easy to pass on to others for their benefit. I have received the inspiration of the higher knowledge of the ages because of my unceasing search for truth and resolution to adversity.

In another dream I am playing some sort of game with my sister and we are talking about how the affirmations are changing our life. I tell her of an incident where I overcame adversity. (See how I'm actually playing this all out in my total sleep now.) In my dream, I tell her that someone was screaming at me and smashing me with the refrigerator door. Within the dream a voice says, "You mean someone assaulted you with the refrigerator door?" And I say, "No, it was a dream"—while I am still dreaming! I recognize this voice is my sentinel to clue me into making a change, so in my dream I say to my attacker, "This doesn't work anymore. You have to stop!" Then the dream changes to another scene and some music is playing in the background that I immediately recognize as a song I used to sing to get up the courage to tell someone to get out of my life or to shape up—in no uncertain terms.(Nazareth-"Hair of the Dog".) I'm grooving on this music and saying to my sister, I can't believe you still have this music. It's been so many years since I heard it, when suddenly I'm overtaken! My eyes are covered and I can't breathe or see and someone is trying to enter my body. This time instead of being unable to make a noise, I scream out "You can't do this to me anymore!"

I woke from this dream and felt stunned at the power of the new affirmations in resolving my nightmares even in my deepest sleep state. I am winning!

One of the solutions that kept coming up in my dreams was the need for me to get out of all caustic relationships. It took enormous courage to act this out in my life but I knew I couldn't heal until I did.

Now in my total subconscious sleep, my mind knows that I now control my dreams! *I now dream that I am dreaming, and often comment to myself within the dream that "I am aware I am dreaming"—which is a lucid dream technique.* This is part of the lucid dreaming affirmations that I did years ago from Frank Young's tape. They were only recently liberated by my affirmation that "All my positive affirmations are a permanent part of me and are recycled on a conscious and subconscious level as needed."

All of these new resolutions to old nightmares are a result of the dream affirmations! The unresolved dreams could resurface for resolution and I understood them.

Application: See appendix D: Goals & Affirmations for a few of my dream affirmations. You can come up with some of your own. Use these affirmations to help you resolve nightmares. They work!

If you don't have nightmares, but are looking for more insight into your subconscious mind and you desire to live out your goals and dreams in your sleep, use the appropriate affirmations from the list and make up some of your own tailored to your goals.

Now watch how your life unfolds to yield up the rewards and success that has eluded you before!

Exercise: Write down the theme of some of your recurring dreams. Search for their deeper meaning. You can find information on dream symbols on the internet.

____

____

____

____

____

Aromatherapy For The Body, Mind, And Emotions

By Phoenix Alexander-Certified Aromatherapist

© 2012, 2020 All Rights Reserved

Aromatherapy is the skilled use of concentrated, pure botanical essential oils for the mind, body, and environment.

DISCLAIMER: This publication is designed for blending perfumes and is suggested for esthetical purposes only. It is intended to be used for therapeutic purposes, and is not intended to be a substitute for traditional medical care. Please consult your physician for any medical conditions you may have.

No claim is made as to the effectiveness of essential oils for treating specific conditions. The remedies contained herein are from herbal texts and scientific research. Author and publisher assume no responsibility for the application and use of this information. The user assumes all risks and responsibility.

Application: One of the most powerful and fascinating ways to release trauma and overcome our emotional responses to adversity, difficulty, and stress is through Aromatherapy.

This ancient art and science is gaining in popularity in the United States

It has been practiced in Europe for a long time.

Have you ever noticed how powerful the sense of smell can be in triggering a long forgotten memory? Perhaps cinnamon reminds you of your grandmother baking oatmeal cookies, or the scent of a perfume stirs memories and feelings about an old lover, or lost loved one. This ability of scent to trigger our memories and emotions can be a vital link in your healing process. Research indicates it is twice as easy to recall a memory of an experience if it is also associated with a smell. This can be incredibly powerful when used in conjunction with somatic memory release bodywork, or when you intentionally anchor a pleasant experience or state of mind to a smell.

I use scent to increase memory retention when I'm studying for a test. I use an essential oil that increases mental stimulation and memory such as peppermint or basil, and each time I study I diffuse the scent or wear it under my nose (diluted of course). Then when I go to take the exam, I wear the scent again. This gives me access to another portion of my brain that processes scent and deals with memory. It gives me an additional tool to help me remember what I've studied.

I made up Aromatherapy necklaces from gems and crystals with a reservoir for holding essential oils. I can wear the essential oil in the form of a beautiful necklace. I made up a custom blend of relaxing massage oil for each of my children and use it when I give them a massage. I've done this since they were toddlers. When they have grown and left the house I can give them the recipe to stimulate powerful, loving, bonding memories of being together. Perhaps they will want to use it for their children. I diffuse specific oils during holidays, like Christmas and Valentine's Day to create special scent memories.

When I am going to do a public speech or seminar, I wear Jasmine oil, because it boosts my confidence and make me feel like a million bucks.

As a Certified Aromatherapist, the use of essential oils and Aromatherapy has filled my life with a sense of wonder and gratitude for yet one other way to access and release traumatic memories and help us to control and even manipulate our feelings and mood.

I use Aromatherapy to help to manage my own emotions and change my mood. I also use it for my family to help promote harmony. I am highly intrigued with the ability to access memory with scent and I'm finding more ways to use this in my healing process and for the relief of the clients who come to see me.

If you have trouble waking up, and getting yourself going, try diffusing some stimulating oils like peppermint, spearmint, or rosemary in the morning instead of relying on that cup of coffee.

Essential Oils are Used Very Effectively in Hospitals in England and the United States

- They are used in air fresheners and diffusers to kill antibiotic resistant strains of bacteria and viruses.

- In England they are used as sedatives for calming patients, pre-and post operative, and to address physical and emotional trauma.

- They are applied in massage and with a diffuser for pain killing properties

- If you have to spend time in the hospital take essential oils with you. You can take a potpourri pot, fill it with water, heat it, and add 15 drops of anti-viral and calming oils. My favorite blend is 5 drops lavender, 4 drops bergamot, 4 drops clove, and 3 drops cinnamon. Alternately, make a room spray with directions found in methods of application.

Aromatherapy has fantastic applications in the workplace, home, schools, etc.

Essential oils can be used to:

- Decrease illness

- Increase production

- Improve concentration and memory retention

- Change or influence mood.

- Research from Japan's largest fragrance manufacturer showed that keyboard operators had about **1/4 fewer input errors** when the air was diffused with lavender. They had about **1/3 fewer errors** when the air was diffused with jasmine, and a whopping **1/2 fewer errors** when the air was diffused with lemon.

- At a training class on Aveda products the instructor presented information on Aveda's essential oil research with children. It showed that using essential oils affects children's mood and influenced their calmness and attention span. They diffused **synthetic lavender** into the air and it caused increased rate of heartbeat, increased perspiration, and fluctuation in brain activity. **Real lavender caused just the opposite effect.** It had a calming effect, decreased perspiration, and normalized heartbeat and brain activity.

- At a class on Aromatherapy the instructor presented information on research that measured the vibrational energy emitted from foods, herbs, and essential oils and compared them. They are measured in megahertz (MHz).

- Viruses have very low vibrational energy and if our energy is low, we are more susceptible to them.

- Food emits the next highest level of vibrational energy, up to 20 MHz.

- Herbs emit a higher vibrational energy level than food, up to 30 MHz.

- Some essential oils emit up to 72 MHz. Using essential oils increases the vibrational energy in our bodies and helps us to resist environmental stresses and illness. They act like a protective shield. Essential oils are up to 100 times more concentrated than dried herbs.

- Kirlian photography, which shows the energy emitted from people and objects, *documents the energy that radiates from essential oils.*

- Use of essential oil increases oxygen in the air and in the blood level by 20%.

I suggest that knowledge of some essential oils and their properties are of vital importance to improving the quality of your life.

Aromatherapy has been scientifically proven to help the mind and body. It's a powerful avenue to healing on every level. I use it in conjunction with bodywork and almost every other aspect of my environment.

I have experienced very powerful physical and emotional healing through the use of essential oils. I have studied the properties of essential oils extensively and have compiled a thorough list of emotional and mental properties of essential oils for you to use and experiment with. I have also included some of the properties for your ailments, skin care, hair care, and perfumery. It is my hope that you will turn to nature and use this knowledge to enhance your life and facilitate complete healing.

Using Aromatherapy and Essential Oils Can Be Very Simple

I suggest using essential oils directly through inhalation (even right out of the bottle) to be a very effective way to start. Because essential oils are so concentrated, one drop can be very effective all by itself. Also, see the page of different methods of application. You will find some favorites. Once you experience the subtle, yet powerful properties of Aromatherapy you will open up new channels of fun, creativity, and improved health.

Benefits of Aromatherapy:

- Reduce stress, and fatigue

- Increase mental alertness and productiveness

- Increase feelings of self-confidence

- Reduce pain and spasm

- Help to balance or change your feelings and emotions

- Increase emotional and physical health

- Improve immune response

- Induce relaxation and calmness

- Increase retention of information

- Create scent anchors or triggers of special memories

- Speed healing responses

- Energize you

- Increase intimacy and sexual responsiveness

- Increase awareness of self and emotions

- Help relieve depression, anxiety, and mood swings.

A Word of Caution: Be an informed consumer. Purchase essential oils and Aromatherapy products from a reputable supplier. Some companies are selling products that are not natural botanical scents and calling it "Aromatherapy." A product only has to contain 5% natural substance to be legally labeled as "pure and natural." Even real essential oils are sometimes cut or adulterated with other oils to reduce cost.

Some of the frequently adulterated oils are Melissa, Lavender, and Neroli. There are also various grades or qualities of oils. Some have more therapeutic value than others. When you are trying to influence emotion, it is especially important to get a high grade and quality essential oil. Please don't confuse this with the fact that essential oils are highly concentrated and must be diluted with some type of carrier (like an oil, bath salt, or milk) when you make it into a specific product. You want it to be pure essential oil to start with.

Essentials of Aromatherapy:

Essential oils are concentrated extracts from roots, wood, leaves, seeds, herbs, fruit, and flowers of aromatic plants. Unless it is derived exclusively from one plant, with no chemical or synthetic additives, it is not an essential oil. Chemically derived fragrances, although pleasing, offer none of the therapeutic and subtle qualities found in real essential oils. All essential oils are antiseptic; some are also antiviral, antibiotic, and anti-fungal. Some affect the nervous system, digestive system, lungs, the brain and glandular systems etc. Essential oils are highly fragrant and evaporate easily.

The term "oil" is a little misleading, as essential oils are not really oils like a vegetable oil. Extracting essential oils is very laborious as large amounts of plant material yield small amounts of oil. Oils, like Eucalyptus, Tea Tree, and Orange have a relative high yield of essential oil in comparison to the plant material needed to make it. However, it takes 5,000 Jasmine flowers to make 1 pound of absolute of Jasmine, 1000 pounds of chamomile flowers to produce 1 pound of Chamomile Essential Oil, and 5,000 pounds of red rose petals—which are picked just after the morning dew when the fragrance is at its peak—to make 1 pound of Rose Essential Oil.

Historically many ancient cultures have used essential oils and aromatic plants for healing, in religion and ceremony, and skin care and perfumery. Modern use of plant oils began in 1928 when a French chemist, Rene Maurice Gattefosse, burned his arm in a chemical explosion in his lab. He plunged his arm into a nearby container of pure lavender Oil. The arm healed astonishingly quickly with no scarring. This led Gattefosse to study and document the properties and uses of essential oils for the rest of his life. He coined the word "aromatherapy".

Internationally, essential oils are often used by Holistic Practitioners and Medical Doctors for the treatment of physical and emotional ailments, and to boost immunity and increase overall health. They are prescribed as medicines and used as a replacement for, or in conjunction with allopathic medicine. In the past few years, America has been introduced to Aromatherapy first in skin and hair care and then in massage. In the future, we may see them used in medical treatment. Currently, the FDA has not approved essential oils for medical applications.

Scent is processed by entering the olfactory nerve receptors in our nose and traveling directly to the limbic system in the mid-brain. This limbic system is directly involved with processing emotions and memories. Our brains link a particular smell to a particular memory and completely bypass the logical thinking areas of the brain.

We have all had the experience of smelling a certain scent that triggers a memory or perhaps just a feeling in us. This tie to our emotions makes Aromatherapy ideal for affecting our mood. Essential oils alter mood by either sedating or stimulating the nervous system. Some act on specific emotions.

The part of the plant from which the oil is extracted gives us clues as to its most effective applications. For instance, oils like Eucalyptus, which are extracted from the leaves where the plant "breathes", are excellent for lung complaints. Oils from the roots help to "ground" us or make us feel balanced and confident. Oils like Neroli, Lavender, Jasmine, and Rose, which are extracted from flowers, have uplifting qualities that help us cope with emotions like grief, depression, and anxiety.

We are bombarded daily with thousands of chemical and synthetic scents manufactured in laboratories that never had anything to do with plants

This can desensitize us to the subtleties of real scents from plant origin. Chemically manufactured scents have no therapeutic value and often contribute to allergies and respiratory over-sensitivity. Using essential oils helps to refine our sense of smell and increase our ability to detect natural fragrances.

Scent plays a strong role in sexual attraction. Men and women produce chemical messages called pheromones that are attractive to the opposite sex. The person's individual smell can be a strong factor in attraction and mate selection. Aromatherapy can have aphrodisiac qualities because these scent messengers are processed in the brain in the same region where sexual drives are regulated.

Endorphins are natural painkillers and can create feelings of euphoria and increased sexual desire. They are produced from the stimulation of the pituitary gland, which is where aphrodisiac scents are processed. The pituitary regulates other endocrine glands such as the thyroid, adrenal glands, and the sexual glands, which is the master gland.

People who are depressed generally have a poor sense of smell and a low sex drive. Increasing our capacity to smell through the use of Aromatherapy is an important benefit.

Consequently, it can also improve sexual communication. Scent memories are a strong factor in sexual arousal, and the enjoyment of sexual experiences. You can use essential oils to create special scent memories of your romantic interludes. Then whenever you smell that scent again a cascade of pleasant feelings and emotions will be triggered.

Sedative oils stimulate the brain to release serotonin, a naturally calming neuro-chemical. Stimulating oils trigger the production of noradrenalin that wakes up your system. The amygdala, an area in the brain, is stimulated by scent and is not accessible by auditory stimulation. This means a scent can trigger a memory that is not accessible through speech.

The hippocampus is also stimulated through scent and is a storage site of memories that along with the amygdala plays a strong role in processing our emotions. As you can plainly see there is nothing mystical about the way scent can influence memory and emotion. It's strictly scientific. It gives us a wonderful natural tool to approach the control of our emotions without harsh prescriptions.

Massage is a very effective application of Aromatherapy. During an aromatherapy massage, the essential oils are absorbed by the lungs through inhalation and into the skin through the pores. They circulate through the body for several hours before being eliminated.

Extensive Knowledge of Essential Oils and Their Properties Is Needed to Effectively Evaluate and Respond to the Needs of the Massage Client.

It is wise to get an Aromatherapy massage from a licensed massage therapist, who has a lot of practice with essential oils or who is a certified Aromatherapist. A Certified Aromatherapist can design Custom Essential Oil blends best suited to your personality and physical health.

Aromatherapy massage oil can be used to apply essential oils whenever you need a treatment not just in conjunction with a massage. Use massage oil after a shower to seal in moisture and give you the benefit of the essential oils. Massage oil can simply mean that vegetable oil is the carrier and you rub it into your skin to spread around the essential oils.

CAUTION should be used when using Essential Oils.

Keep out of reach of children and pets. Always use diluted, except in an "aromatic diffuser". Consult an Aromatherapist or Aromatherapy book to see which oils are safe if you have any of the following conditions: Epilepsy, pregnancy or nursing, high or low blood pressure, asthma, cancer, sensitive skin, or allergic reactions. Babies and young children should not use certain oils. All oils must be diluted to 1/2 to 1/3 the adult concentration.

WARNING: I NEVER RECOMMEND TAKING ESSENTIAL OILS INTERNALLY.

Everyday Uses for Aromatherapy:

For the Mind and Body--

- A drop of essential oil in the hair will keep it delightfully fragrant all day. Oils such as Jasmine, and Rose, are confidence builders. Patchouli, YlangYlang, and Sandalwood are reputed aphrodisiacs.

- Get an Aromatherapy massage with essential oil massage blends to suit your mood, personality, and physical health.

- Bath salts blended with essential oils for their therapeutic qualities can enhance relaxation and give you an "attitude adjustment" or address a physical condition.

- Essential oils greatly enhance skin and hair care products. Use them in cleansers, toners, and facial oils for moisturizing. They can be made specifically to suit your skin and hair type (dry hair, dandruff, sensitive skin, mature skin, etc.).

- Essential oil "body oils" can be used before or after the bath for nourishing and moisturizing the skin.

Lift Your Mood While Cleaning:

- A few drops of your favorite essential oil added to the dish soap will undoubtedly make washing dishes a more pleasant chore. Add the essential oil to the soap and then add the water. (Essential oils are not water-soluble and need a "carrier" or "emulsifier" like soap, to disperse them evenly in whatever application you are using them. Always add essential oils to the carrier or emulsifier first and then to the water.) Recommended essential oils: Citrus Oils, Lavindin, Mints, Cinnamon, Clove, (spice oils).

- Add a few drops of oil to your mop water with whatever cleanser or soap you use to clean the floor. Recommended oils: Mints, Citrus Oils, Lavindin, Anise, and spice oils.

- A few drops of oils like Lavindin, Mints, Cedarwood, or Bergamot add a fresh, fragrant touch to your laundry. Add them to the final rinse cycle of the washer in the last few minutes and agitate them around with your hand to disperse the oils. Or put a few drops on a cotton cloth and toss it in the dryer the last few minutes of the cycle.

Environmental Fragrancing: Enhance Your Environment Through Scent:

- Put a few drops of essential oils on the cardboard of the toilet paper roll to give it some antiseptic qualities as well as a pleasing scent to your bathroom.

- Lavender and Rosemary can be made into sachets to repel moths from your clothing. They are also good for shock and trauma. Keep a sachet in your purse, car, or in your desk.

⊘ Use essential oils in your homemade potpourri. It's usually more economical than commercial fragrance oil because of its concentration. Commercial potpourri fragrances are synthetic and chemically derived unlike natural essential oil fragrances that give the added benefit of being antiseptic and working on the emotional and physical planes to enhance your wellness.

Using natural fragrances can actually boost your immunity and your sense of smell. Synthetic perfumes and fragrances are a major cause of allergies, and even headaches.

⊘ Scent your stationery by adding a drop of oil to a tissue and storing it in a closed container with the stationery. Your recipient will be delighted to get a letter from you. It will capture the memory of your letter with scent.

⊘ Essential oils can be diffused into the air in an "aromatic diffuser" which breaks up the molecules of the essential oil and disperses them over larger areas than they would reach without the diffuser. Essential oil blends can be made for the diffuser to treat many specific conditions such as lethargy, headache, anxiety, or to fight viruses and bacteria.

⊘ A diffuser at the office can increase productivity, improve concentration, and fight germs. In the bedroom, aphrodisiac blends can be diffused to create a luxurious romantic mood. Try diffusing some lively oils during exercise to open up the lungs and stimulate your mind and muscles.

The Possibilities Are Endless!

Aromatherapy Methods of Application

- **Massage Oil** for a full body treatment (regular dose): 45-60 drops in 4 ounces of high quality "carrier" vegetable oil such as Jojoba Oil, sesame, grapeseed, or sweet almond oil. Use a cold-pressed oil for best results. Essential oils must always be diluted in a carrier or emulsifier and usually used in a 2% - 5% concentration.

Jojoba oil is the closest to the skin's natural oil, sebum, and does not oxidize or go rancid like many vegetable oils.

- **Massage oil for a local area** (specific dose) such as a sore shoulder. 45 to 60 drops in 2 ounces of vegetable oil.

- **Bath:** 6 to 12 drops per bath diluted first in a carrier such as 1 Tbsp. of milk, vegetable oil, or liquid soap. Add essential oils and carrier after water is drawn and just before you get in the bath. Alternately, make a bath salts combination with 2 Tbsp. Sea Salt, 2 Tbsp. Baking Soda, and 2 Tbsp. Epsom Salt with 10 drops essential oil. Add to bath just before entering. Don't turn on a fan or keep the door open or the vapors will escape. Use only 3-5 drops of essential oils for children.

- **Inhalation:** Take a sniff directly from a bottle of essential oils, be careful not to get directly on skin. Alternately, add 5-12 drops essential oils to a bowl of hot water. Hold head over bowl, cover head, and bowl with a towel, and inhale.

- **Toning Body Mist:** 2-1/2 % dilution. Use 60 to 75 drops of essential oils mixed with 2 Tbsp. Witch Hazel (an herbal astringent available at drug stores) or Vodka. Fill a 4 oz. spray top container, with essential oils and dispersant. Then fill remainder of bottle with purified water. You can use this as a delicious toning mist on the body. Spray it on several times a day to revive and refresh you. In the summer, refrigerate it and spray on the cooling mist.

- **Air Spray:** 5% dilution. For environmental fragrancing or sickroom, use a 4 ounce bottle with a spray top. Add 3 ounce of purified water then mix 120-150 drops of essential oils with a dispersant such as vodka or witch hazel (about 1Tbsp.). Add enough water to fill the rest of the container. Spray frequently in sick room.

- **Aromatic Sheet Hydrotherapy Treatment:** Mix 15 drops of essential oils with 12 ounces of very warm water in a spray bottle. Lay a large plastic shower curtain or covering on the bed or comfortable surface. Spray a cotton sheet with essential oil and water mixture. Immediately lay down onto the cotton sheet and wrap yourself completely in it. Have someone lay a wool blanket or large cotton bath towel over the top of you. Relax and enjoy a detoxifying, relaxation treatment for 20 to 30 minutes. This can be used to great effect for decreasing nervousness and shock. Alternately, use very cold water following the sheet treatment to boost your immune system, detoxify, and act as a general tonic.

☍ **Diffuser:** Several types of diffuser are available. Some use a small candle to heat a small basin filled with water and several drops of essential oils. Some heat electrically (like those "plug-in air fresheners" or potpourri pots). For maximum effectiveness, use one that breaks the essential oil molecule apart and pumps it into the air without the use of heat. The types that warm essential oils may decrease the therapeutic effectiveness of the essential oils. Small clay glazed pottery with corks are available to fill with essential oils and diffuse the oils out over time. You can find these at health food stores with Aromatherapy sections.

☍ **Moisturizing Mask:** Mix 1 Tbsp. plain yogurt; with active cultures, with 1Tbsp. dry oatmeal, and 1 teaspoon honey. Add 3 drops of essential oils. Apply to face and relax for 20 minutes. Rinse off and enjoy a softly moisturized face. Recommended Essential oils: Lavender, Neroli, Rose, Chamomile, Rosemary, Benzoin, and Rosewood.

Contraindications and Cautions:

- Cancer and Chemotherapy—NO AROMATHERAPY

- Epilepsy—Avoid: Sage, Sweet Fennel, Hyssop, Basil, Tarragon

- Pregnancy & Lactation—Greater dilutions, only a few safe oils are Safe

Essential Oils for Pregnancy:

Bergamot, Caraway, Chamomile, Citronella, Clove, Eucalyptus, Frankincense, Jasmine, Lavender, Lemongrass, Mandarin, Neroli, Orange, Sandalwood, Tangerine, Tea Tree, YlangYlang, Nutmeg, Vetiver

In Pregnancy Avoid: Aniseed, Basil, Clary Sage (until labor), Cinnamon, Cypress, Fennel, Hyssop, Juniper, Marjoram, Mugwort, Myrrh, Oregano, Pennyroyal, Peppermint, Rosemary, Sage, Savory, Tarragon, Wintergreen

Avoid For The Following Health Concerns:

- High Blood Pressure—Avoid: Rosemary, Peppermint, Hyssop, Thyme, Sage

- Low Blood Pressure—Avoid: Clary Sage, Lavender, YlangYlang

- Asthma—Be cautious of using diffusers

- Babies and Children—Only a few safe oils. Use in 1/3 to 1/2 adult dose

- Sensitive Skin or Allergies—Avoid: Basil, Lemon, Melissa, Peppermint, Thyme, Cinnamon, Lemongrass

- Using Homeopathic Remedies—Avoid: Camphor, Mints, Eucalyptus, Thyme, and more aggressive/stimulating oils

Some Essential Oils, Their Properties, and Indications

Definition of Terms:

- Analgesic—relieves pain
- Antiseptic—destroys or inhibits the growth of bacteria, germs
- Antispasmodic—relieves spasm in muscles
- Astringent—tightens tissues
- Cytophylactic—stimulates cell growth
- Diuretic—decreases water retention
- Stomachic—stomach tonic, used in stomach disorders
- Tonic—giving tone to the body generally, mildly invigorating

Basil: Mental/memory stimulant, tonic, uplifting, and antidepressant. Use for nervous tension, hysteria, insomnia, and mental fatigue. A stimulant of adrenal cortex. Use for: Migraine, fainting, earache, nausea, chronic cold, and vomiting.

Birch (is like wintergreen.): Invigorating to the body and mind. Anti-spasmodic, detoxifying, diuretic. Skin care: Use for cellulitis.

Benzoin: Decreases anxiety, eases sorrow. Good for deep emotional healing. Balances Energy. Regulates secretions. Good for cough, laryngitis, urinary infections. Skin Care: Cracked, chapped irritated skin, rashes and wound healing. Helps essential oil massage blends to be absorbed in skin. Perfumery: Major oil--Fixative.

Bergamot: Refreshing, relaxing, uplifting, emotional balancer. Decreases anxiety, soothes fear, grounding.

Cedarwood: Boosts energy. Good for anxiety and fear, deep relaxation, sedative, grounding. Antiseptic, anti-fungal.

Chamomile: Calming, anti-depressant. Treats nervous tension, anger, and insomnia. Great oil for children—use for tantrums. Anti-inflammatory, antibiotic, good for pain (especially stomach pain). Skin Care: Sensitive skin, inflamed skin. Hair Care: Normal and blonde hair. Perfumery: Middle to top note.

Cinnamon Leaf: Aphrodisiac—use in inhalations only. Highly antiseptic, antiviral, antibiotic, skin irritant in high concentrations. Stimulates circulation and fights infectious diseases. Great in potpourri.

Clary Sage: "Oil of laughter". Aphrodisiac, anti-depressant, balances emotions, euphoric, decreases fear and depression and paranoia. Promotes grounding and a supported feeling. Helps overcome poor memory and insomnia. Good for Dreamwork. Increases female creativity. Cytophylactic. Skin Care: Normal, mature, and dry skin; skin balancer. Perfumery: Base to middle note. Avoid in the first five months of pregnancy.

Clove: Aphrodisiac, intellectual stimulant, and respiratory stimulant. Highly antiseptic, antibiotic, antiviral, analgesic, stomachic. Good for toothache and inflamed gums. Use for sore throat. Great in potpourri. Skin irritant in high doses.

Cypress: Good for: Emotional grounding, mental concentration. Antispasmodic, diuretic, lymph tonic, varicosities, and urinary infections. Skin care: Oily and over-hydrated skin, astringent, and soothing in small doses. Perfumery: Middle note used in aftershaves. Avoid if pregnant.

Eucalyptus Citriodora: Sedative, calming. Antiseptic, antiviral, insect repellant, deodorizer, disinfectant. Good for: Arthritis, rheumatism, lung and sinus congestion.

Eucalyptus Totem: Respiration, antiviral, expectorant. Use for urinary tract infections, insect bites, and sinus complaints. Skin care: Cleansing, purifying, treats acne.

Frankincense: Great for healing old emotional wounds like abuse issues, traumas, and childhood issues. Brings power and a sense of belonging. Soothes fear. Emotional balancer. Calming, grounding. Good for lengthening and opening breathing, antiseptic, good for healing infected wounds, dries excess mucous. Skin Care: Cell regenerator, mature skin, and wrinkles. Perfumery: Base note and enhancer.

Geranium: Emotional balancer. Can be uplifting or sedating at the same time, depending on what your body needs. Antiseptic, diuretic, female hormone balancer. Skin care: astringent, cell regeneration, wound healing, cuts, burns, aged or chapped skin. Perfumery: middle to top note.

Grapefruit: Emotionally uplifting and clearing, refreshing. Diuretic, drainer, digestive stimulant. Skin care: Astringent, oily skin. Perfumery: Middle to top note.

Jasmine: "Be good to yourself oil" antidepressant, euphoric, aphrodisiac, uplifting, increases sexual confidence and self esteem, eases depression, relieves insomnia. Skin care: Moisturizer good for dry and sensitive skin. Perfumery: fixative to middle note.

Juniper: Memory and brain stimulant. Relieves fatigue. arthritis, anti-inflammatory, diuretic. Skin care: Dermatitis, hair loss.

Lavender: "Universal Oil" because it helps with so many things. Balances emotions, eases nervous exhaustion, and depression. Calming, reduces anger. Good for trauma and shock. Works on nearly everything, burns, bug bites, headaches, antiseptic, antiviral, antibiotic, anti-fungal, antispasmodic. Research indicates that lavender may increase erectile response in men. Skin care: Heals wounds, may prevent scarring from burns, cuts and abrasions. Increases cell regeneration. Use for sensitive skin or acne, and helps heal eczema. Perfumery: Middle to top note.

Lavindin: Use when you don't need the subtle emotional effects that lavender gives. Deodorizer, insect repellant, antiseptic, and analgesic. Skin care: Cleansing.

Lemon: Antidepressant, uplifting, eases anxiety, memory stimulant. Antiseptic, diuretic, immune-stimulant, anti-viral, anti-fungal, tonic. Skin care: Astringent. Use for cold sores, eczema. Use in small concentrations on skin. Avoid if you have sensitive skin.

Lemon Thyme: Soothing, healing, uplifting, stimulant. Use for: Depression and nervous weakness. Antiseptic, antibiotic, tonic, calming to irritable bowels. Skincare: Good for all skin types, acne, oily, infections. Avoid in pregnancy.

Lime: Tonic, antidepressant, uplifting, eases anxiety. Antiseptic, antibiotic, stimulant, digestive stimulant, lymphatic stimulant. Perfumery: Middle to top note, used in aftershaves.

Marjoram: "The Plant Tranquilizer." Calming, good for stress, insomnia, grief, disappointment, and loneliness. Helps increase self-confidence. May decrease sex drive. Lowers blood pressure, antispasmodic for digestive system, menstrual stimulant. Skin care: Good for all skin types, especially sensitive skin. Perfumery: Middle note. Avoid in the first three months of pregnancy.

Myrrh: Has properties similar to Frankincense. Use for sore throat, infected gums. Perfumery: Fixative to base note.

Neroli: Antidepressant, aphrodisiac, sedative, comforting, calming. Good for insomnia, hysteria, emotional shock, grief, and nervous tension, and stress. Skin care: sensitive skin. Perfumery: Top note.

Orange: Good for heartache, hysteria, and insomnia, uplifting, antidepressant, euphoric, lightens mood. Great oil for children. Digestive stimulant, diuretic, Skin care: dry or mature skin. Perfumery: Middle note, extender.

Patchouli: Good for heartache, insomnia, disappointment. Tonic, sedative, aphrodisiac, euphoric, lightens mood, lifts self-esteem. Anti-fungal, antiseptic, antibiotic, cell regenerator, deodorant. Skin care: Dry, chapped, inflamed, acne. Perfumery: Fixative to middle.

Peppermint: Antidepressant, tonic, mental stimulant, aphrodisiac, refreshing, relieves fatigue. Stomachic. Stimulates the lungs and nervous system. Use for headaches, fever, colds, flu, nausea, asthma, bronchitis, sinusitis. Skin care: Use for acne, dermatitis, and itchy skin. Avoid if you have sensitive skin or high blood pressure. Perfumery: Top note.

Pettigrain: Sedative, refreshing, decreases mental fatigue, and confusion. Helps treat poor memory. Antispasmodic, digestive aid, treats flatulence. Skin care: excellent for oily and acne skin. Perfumery: Major oil, middle note extender.

Pine: Tonic, sedative, comforting, eases anxiety, and stress, eases fatigue. Expectorant. Perfumery: Middle to top note.

Rose: "Oil of the heart", aphrodisiac, uplifting, and antidepressant. Use for deep emotional pain and emotional shock, grief, low self-esteem, insomnia. May increase forgiveness, and compassion. Helps stimulate confidence. Calming, tonic, female hormone regulator. Skin care: Good for sensitive, inflamed skin, broken capillaries, mature skin. Perfumery: Top note.

Rosemary: Antidepressant, uplifting, refreshing, strengthening. Stimulates brain and memory. Good for low energy, mental strain. Reduces anger. Highly antiseptic, tonic, analgesic, stimulant. Skin care: Cell regenerator. Use for: Acne, dermatitis, dry, mature, or wrinkled skin. Perfumery: Middle note. Avoid if you have high blood pressure or are pregnant.

Rosewood: Antidepressant, uplifting, emotional balancer. Use for: Sorrow, headache, nausea. Great in skin care: Cell regenerator, antiseptic, acne, dermatitis wrinkles, mature skin, dry, flaky skin. Perfumery: Middle note.

Sandalwood: Used most for fatigue, depression, grounding, anxiety, aphrodisiac, strengthening, tonic. Corresponds to male pheromone. Antiseptic, antiviral, wound healer, urinary tract infections. Skin care: Soothing, moisturizing, cell regenerator. Use for dry, cracked mature skin. Perfumery: Major oil, base to middle note.

Spearmint: Stimulant to mind and body, uplifting. Decreases mental fatigue. Use for headache, sinusitis, depression, fatigue, mental strain. Skin care: Cleansing, acne, and dermatitis. Perfumery: Top note.

Spruce: Mental reflection, and decreasing fatigue and stress. Antispasmodic. Good for rheumatism, lungs, Perfumery: Middle to top.

Tangerine: Most sedative of citrus oils, great for children. Soothing and refreshing. Use for: Nervous tension, grief, hysteria. Helpful in stimulation of the sexual chakra. Antispasmodic, Perfumery: Middle note.

Tea Tree (Melaleuca): One of the most versatile oils. Antiseptic, anti-fungal, antiviral, antibiotic, used for nearly everything. Can be used without diluting. Use for: Candida, athlete's foot, lymphatic drainage. Good for acute conditions such as wounds, insect bites, etc. Skin care: All skin types, especially acne, dandruff.

Vetiver: Comforting, grounding, eases stress, and anxiety. Use for: Arthritis, rheumatism, boosts immune system, works on intestinal system. Perfumery: major oil, fixative to base note.

YlangYlang: "Flower of Flowers" Antidepressant, sedative, aphrodisiac, euphoric, calming. Use for: Anger, stress, disappointment, insomnia, impotence, and frigidity. Good for nervousness. Antispasmodic. Reduces high blood pressure. Skin care: Good for hair growth and oily skin. Perfumery: Fixative.

Aromatherapy Recipes

Massage Oils:

To create the various types of massage oils, add the following essential oils to two ounces of vegetable oil:

Invigorating Massage Oil:

- 17 drops Rosewood
- 6 drops Orange
- 2 drops Geranium

Relaxing Massage Oil:

- 13 drops Lavender
- 2 drops Geranium
- 10 drops Sandalwood

Aromatherapy Baths:

Add the essential oils to 2 tablespoons of a "carrier" such as sea salt or powdered milk. Add to bath just before entering.

Uplifting Aromatherapy Bath

- 2 drops Clary Sage
- 2 drops Bergamot
- 2 drops YlangYlang

Sleep Inducing Bath

- 7 drops Lavender
- 3 drops Marjoram
- 1 drop Chamomile

Immunity Stimulant Bath

- 5 drops Tea Tree
- 2 drops Lemon
- 3 drops Eucalyptus
- 1 drop Thyme
- 3 drops Lavender

Stress Relief Bath

- 3 drops Marjoram
- 2 drops Bergamot
- 2 drops YlangYlang
- 2 drops Orange
- 1 drop Pettigrain
- 1 drop Neroli (optional)

Appendix A: Code of Conduct Statement

Each choice I make is governed by my values as set forth in this statement:

- Happiness, peace, and living true principles, are the object and design of my existence.

- I recognize that true peace comes from living with honor, dignity, and truth.

- I never violate my personal ethics for the approval of others, for temporary gain, comfort, satisfaction, or for the sake of "keeping the peace".

- I never allow anyone to violate my body or my personal boundaries.

- I devote my life to: Learning; sharing; growing; overcoming all fears, limitations, and obstacles; and exercising compassion and mercy for others, while experiencing love and joy.

- I seek to lift the burdens of others, to share my knowledge, and teach true principles through example, recognizing that my strength comes from the Lord and is inexhaustible.

- I accept responsibility for my own problems only and teach others to do the same.

- I let my light shine forth to all the world.

- I live with balance, using my resources wisely to spend most of my time doing things that matter most.

- My stewardship is first to the development of myself spiritually, emotionally, and in all other ways; I then have the wisdom and energy to fulfill my stewardship to my family.

- I recognize that each day is a Gift from God.

- I use the unique abilities and talents the Lord has blessed me with and seek to develop other talents.

- I know that the Lord has, and always will, work all things for my good.

- I move with peace through every experience in my life.

- I quickly seek the "lesson to be learned "in each situation and recognize it as an opportunity for growth.

- All of my life experiences have forged my character into strong, tempered steel.

- I commit myself to excellence in all I do.

- I recognize the strength, majesty, and glory of my spirit and seek to see my whole self in this same way.

- I move with dignity, strength, beauty, and compassion upon the earth.

- I love and honor my body, the temple of my spirit.

- I don't allow the negative labels and opinions of others to influence my positive opinions of myself.

- When others criticize or seek to limit my potential, I ask myself "is this true about me?" If it is, I change it. If it's not, I let it go.

- I choose not to participate in relationships that are deeply destructive, or with people unwilling to participate in a healthy relationship. I protect my children and myself from abusive relationships.

- I teach my children by example what healthy relationships feel like.

- I realize that mistakes are an opportunity for growth and change, not a condemnation. I do not fear mistakes, I use them to improve my life and move forward.

- I do not seek to cover my sins and mistakes instead I correct them and move forward.

- I forgive the mistakes of others.

- I have intrinsic worth and value as a daughter of God. I recognize this same worth in others.

- I have a deep understanding of myself—my motivation, my purpose, and my boundaries. I seek this same understanding of my loved ones.

- Since judgment is necessary for correct decision-making, I seek to judge wisely and compassionately.

- I use my resources wisely, and use money as my servant, not my master.

- I am self-reliant financially, emotionally, physically, and spiritually. I choose to be interdependent with those I love.

I AM INCREDIBLY RESILIENT!

I AM INDOMITABLE!

Appendix B: Life-Improving Affirmations

What you say to yourself repeatedly becomes your reality.

Repeat one affirmation several times per day for one week, then move to the next. Now repeat two affirmations each day, and so on. You will be amazed at the great things that will happen!

- It's easy for me to understand other's feelings.
- Failure only means I'm one step closer to victory.
- I like who I am.
- I'm a winner!
- I'm thankful for the good things in my life.
- I am brilliant!
- I notice and compliment the goodness in others.
- Good and happy things come to me easily.
- I control my own thoughts and emotions.
- Learning is easy!
- I am extraordinary!
- I commit myself to excellence in all I do.
- All things work together for my good!
- I like the way I look.
- I was born to be happy.
- I "talk it out" to solve my problems.
- I set and achieve meaningful goals.
- I'm an important person.
- Within me there is greatness!
- I constantly try to improve myself.
- I talk kindly to others and myself.
- I'm an effective communicator.
- I'm a good influence on others.
- Opposition makes me stronger.
- I am an expert problem solver.

- I have many skills and talents.
- I respect the rights of others.
- I make valuable contributions.
- Peace and prosperity come easily to me.
- I promote success in myself and others!
- I am creating helpful new habits.
- I am relaxed and confident.
- Mistakes are for Learning!
- My life has an important purpose!
- I look for the good in all situations.
- I'm having a great day!
- I make friends easily.
- I open my mind to new opportunities and ideas.
- I look for opportunities to help others.
- I'm a happy person!
- I am cooperative.
- My thoughts are the key to my success.
- Problems help me discover my strengths.
- I am optimistic!
- I love learning.
- My actions make the world a better place.
- I was born to accomplish something great.
- I am creative.
- I'm helpful.
- Good things are constantly happening to me.
- I never give up!
- I'm efficient.

Appendix C: Dream Affirmations

- I am always safe!

- All of my dreams support me in the changes I'm making and are the place where I live my new, happy, prosperous, lifestyle.

- All of my positive affirmations are available to my conscious and subconscious mind and replay as needed for my benefit.

- I always have sentinels and guardians inside my dreams to guide my dreams to a positive conclusion and help me interpret my dreams.

- My dreams are all supportive of the new life I'm creating.

- My dreams are a place for self-discovery where I uncover and resolve blocks that are keeping me from progressing.

- I can easily enter and exit my dreams.

- I can command anyone to leave my dreams.

- I am in a place of power and control in all my dreams.

- My dreams are a place where I live out and enjoy the new lifestyle I am creating for myself.

- All of the old dreams that recycled are now free to surface for resolution.

- The symbols in my dreams are easily recognizable and clearly understood by me.

- I am in control of my dreams even in a subconscious state and can manipulate my dreams to reflect my new life and positive changes.

- My dreams always conclude with a positive, empowering resolution.

- My subconscious mind works in harmony with my goals and affirmations.

- I am progressing exponentially as I take control of my dreams and program my subconscious to support my affirmations and goals.

- I creatively resolve all difficulty and disharmony within my dreams.

- There are limitless possibilities open to me in the positive resolution of conflict or problems within my dreams.

- My vivid imagination comes to my aid in problem solving within my dreams.

- My dreams are a powerful tool in my control to create the life I want to lead.

- I am always in control of the events in my dreams and can manipulate my dreams to work for my highest purposes.

- I am easily able to recall dreams that need resolutions and work through them.

- All my dreams work for my benefit in helping me achieve my goals and ambitions.

Appendix D: Goals & Affirmations Template

Goals and Affirmation For ____________ (month)

Specific Goal	Sun	Mon	Tue	Wed	Thu	Fri	Sat

Affirmations:

____

____

____

____

____

Visualizations:

____

____

____

____

____

Appendix E: Affirmations for Transforming Anger

Confrontation means I have an opportunity to bring up an issue for healthy resolution.

Confrontation is the necessary first step in setting a boundary, and asking for positive change.

Anger is a gift of insight into my needs, beliefs, and thoughts.

The purpose of anger is to move me to take necessary action to meet my needs and change my circumstances and move me into resolution through forgiveness and empathy.

By taking appropriate action when I feel angry, I'm increasing my mind and body wellness and personal empowerment.

I can immediately ground myself repelling any negativity or anger coming toward me and remain balanced, resolute, calm and peaceful inside knowing that I am smart enough to remove myself safely from dangerous situations and have the skills to handle all other circumstances.

I recognize that confrontation is necessary in healthy relationships for each person to constructively ask for change and express their needs and feelings.

I feel comfortable and justified in delivering a well constructed, healthy confrontational message that takes responsibility for my own feelings and asks for change in another person's behavior.

I feel safe in knowing I have the strength and resources to solve any problem I encounter.

Anger is often the feeling that initially gives me the courage and strength to set boundaries and make positive changes.

Even when angry, I can use my words in ways that will most likely bring about successful resolution.

I control the volume of my voice while I'm angry to most effectively deliver my message in a way that it's truly heard.

Anger creates the opportunity for me to gain understanding of my needs and feelings and create positive change in my life.

I can do all things through Christ who strengthens me.

I am always in control of my thoughts and emotions.

When I feel angry it means an important need has been blocked or my personal boundaries have been violated or I thoughts I'm trying to control someone or something that's not in my control.

I recognize that other's needs and feelings are as important to them as mine are to me.

I commit to taking the time to understand the needs and feelings of others.

I realize it's okay if we have differing opinions and viewpoints.

My anger is often generated by the perspective I have of events and the behaviors of others, so I take the time to evaluate if changing the value I place on the event would better serve me.

I'm totally invested in doing my part to create loving, nurturing, harmonious relationships with others.

I'm committed to working through any problem I have with other while recognizing they may choose not to.

I always ask myself when conflict arises "What's my part in this problem?"

I take responsibility for my words and actions and I say I'm sorry when needed.

I feel safe in saying "I could be wrong. Help me understand your point of view."

I always work toward a mutually beneficial situation recognizing I may need to compromise some of my opinions or needs.

I can respectfully discuss problems and my feelings while controlling the volume of my voice.

I can state my need and feelings assertively and ask for change.

I can create inner calmness even in turbulent times.

I communicate my needs in a constructive way.

My anger can be used to improve my situation or relationship if I handle it correctly.

I can at any time choose to drop my anger and replace it with forgiveness, compassion, understanding and internal peace.

I can take a time out from a conflict, or use a punching bag, or do something physical like take a walk to transform the anger and return at another time with a spirit of cooperation and problem solving.

I recognize I can only be in control of myself, not anyone else.

The most powerful people in the world are those who choose to control themselves.

I trust that I am loved and loveable.

I connect warmly with others.

The quality of my thoughts creates the level of anger or contentment I feel.

As I choose the thoughts I think, which influences my feelings and behavior.

My interpretation of the events and circumstances in my life creates my anger or acceptance of the situation and consequently my level of happiness and satisfaction.

By examining my thoughts and feelings, I can interpret my circumstances in a less angry and more empowering way.

I accept whatever feelings I have while taking the time to evaluate and implement more effective ways of thinking to create the life I choose to live.

I am now creating the life I choose to live with my thoughts, feelings and actions.

The key to using my anger effectively is the way I view things.

I create inner calmness and peace when I use anger to take action that moves me toward healthy empowerment and forgiveness.

I am using my thoughts and feelings to create the happiness, prosperity, abundance and life I deserve.

I am now creating a masterpiece of my life.

As I think of what is creating angry feelings, I can work with my breathing to release it.

I breathe in while thinking of the angry circumstances and hold the breath with the thought for a count of 5 then slowly exhale while releasing the angry feelings and inhale with thoughts and visualizations of tranquility with the next breath.

Although I feel angry at the moment, there are things I'm grateful for about this situation or person. I'm grateful for.....................

I'm brilliant, resilient, indomitable, and skillfully able to resolve any and every problem that I may face.

Anger is a valuable cue that something needs to change.

Everyone has anger in varying degrees of intensity, so it's normal. What I do with my anger determines the quality of my life and relationships.

When I'm angry I first work to release the fight or flight hormones by taking physical action, then I address the emotions until I can get to a state of peace and calm.

Appendix F: Recommended Resources

<u>Prosperity Consciousness-How to Tap Your Unlimited Wealth</u> by Fredric Lehrman. Nightingale Conant, Ill. 1994. *CD's available from Nomad University P.O. Box 5677 Bellevue, WA 98006 $85. postage paid or from www.nomaduniversity.com/store.htm*

Model Mugging Self Defense Training. Find local classes at their website at: http://www.modelmugging.org Look under worldwide courses.

Self Defense Books:

The Safe Zone, a Kid's Guide to Personal Safety. Donna Chaiet and Francine Russell,

Self-Defense for Women, Willy Cahill, Ohara Publications Inc. CA, 1978.

Safe at All Times; Protecting Yourself and Your Family in a Dangerous World, Janet

The Gift of Fear and Other Survival Signals that Protect Us From Violence. Gavin DeBecker,

Obsession- John Douglas and Mark Olshaker

Additional Resources:

I have read each of these books and many of them have helped shaped my feelings, thinking and actions. They may be of value to you too.

What to Say When You Talk to Yourself- Shad Helmstetter Ph.D.

Talking to Yourself- Pamela E Butler

Psycho-Cybernetics- Maxwell Maltz

People Skills- Robert Bolton Ph.D

1001 Ways To Be Romantic- Gregory J.P. Godek

The 7 Habits of Highly Effective People- Stephen R Covey

Uncoupling Turning Point in Intimate Relationships- Diane Vaughan

The Five Languages of Apology- Gary Chapman, Jennifer Thomas

Coming Apart Why Relationships End and How to Live Through the Ending of Yours-

    By Daphne Rose Kingma

Think and Grow Rich Napolean Hill

Dare To Win- Mark Victor Hansen and Jack Canfield

The Power of Positive Thinking- Norman Vincent Peale

Active Parenting Today- Michael H Popkin Ph.D

Men Who Hate Wome & The Women Who Love Them- Dr Susan Forward

The Dance of Anger- Harriet Goldhor Lerner, Ph.D

The Betrayal Bond Breaking Free of Exploitive Relationships- Patrick J Carnes, Ph.D

Avoid Legal Divorce by Avoiding Emotional Divorce- Dr. John Lewis Lund

Do I Have To Give Up Me To Be Loved By You? Jordan Paul, Ph.D, and Margaret Paul Ph.D

Women Who Love Too Much: When you keep Wishing and Hoping He'll Change

     By Robin Norwood

The Slight Edge- Jeff Olson

How to Stop Worrying and Start Living- Dale Carnegie

You Can Heal Your Life- Louise Hay

The Anger Workbook: Les Carter Ph.D, Frank Minerth M.D.

The Gift of Anger: Marcia Cannon Ph.D

Creating Your Own Destiny- Patrick Snow

Why Does he Do That? In the Minds of Angry and Controlling Men- Lundy Bancroft

Making Love Last Forever- Gary Smalley

Aromatherapy Workbook Marcel Lavabre

The Practice of Aromatherapy- Jean Valnet, MD

The Art of Aromatherapy- Robert Tisserand

Aromatherapy for Women- Maggie Tisserand

Herbs and Aromatherapy- Johanna Metcalfe

The Herb Book- John Lust

The Complete Book of Herbs- Lesley Bremness

The Complete Book of Essential Oils and Aromatherapy- Valerie Ann Worwood

Unlimited Power- Anthony Robbins

Lessons From Great Lives- Sterling W Sill, Dan McCormick

Living Your Life in Balance-Shannon S Carlson

Confronting Without Guilt or Conflict- Bob Weyent

As A Man Thinketh- James Allen

Discipline Without Shouting or Spanking- Jerry Wycoff Ph.D, Barbara C Unell

These are Audio programs on CD and Tapes that have shaped my thinking: They may be of value to you.

Action Strategies for Personal Achievement- Brian Tracy

21 Great Ways to Stay In Love Forever- Brian Tracy

21 Great Ways to Meet and Marry The Man of Your Dreams- Brian Tracy

Personal Power- Anthony Robbins

Get The Edge- Anthony Robbins

Attitude is Everything- Paul J Meyer

Create Your Greatest Life- Les Brown

Beyond Scents: Aromatherapy Home Study Course- Michael Scholes

From Victim Into Victor: The Ultimate Guide To Overcoming Trauma, Abuse and PTSD

Companion Book:

As a Trauma Survivor, I have learned many physical practices for healing and getting the disempowering emotions, created the trauma, out of my body. You can too.

I have written a Companion Book for Veterans, and Trauma Survivors. It can give you another 200 pages of invaluable help, including more practices to get well and thrive.

It includes practices like, Qigong, and Acupressure for Emotional and Physical Wellbeing.

I can come to your group of Veterans, or Survivors and teach them hands on skills for not just surviving, but how to get out of a trauma flashback almost immediately.

Buy it on Amazon, or directly from me at the website below.

Additionally you can go to my website for videos and articles on overcoming trauma.

www.FromVictimIntoVictor.org

Here is more about "From Victim Into Victor The Ultimate Guide To Overcoming Trauma, Abuse and PTSD."

My Calling in life is to "Carry the Torch" for other trauma survivors. My experiences have a purpose; besides personal suffering, if they help others to heal! This book is to light the way to your breakthrough in going, "From Victim Into Victor".

I was placed in horrific circumstances so many times! Not because of my own choices, but because of the choices of my perpetrators. I had to decide; do they win, or am I going to exercise my own power to heal and be empowered?

This book is my gift, from the heart, to the world of Trauma Survivors. I am being tremendously vulnerable in sharing the experiences of my life found in this book with you! But I can't help you unless I give it a voice! I have been through nearly every kind of trauma imaginable–AND THEN SOME! I don't share my deepest trauma-- even in this book. There is so much more that I can't share in polite public. But trust me when I say, I am an insider! I know what trauma does!

I want to SAVE LIVES —Not just my own! I want you to have the empowerment tools that you need so that when you are ready to give up on life—*You Won't!*

To go from "Victim into Victor" means you are thriving, productive, and happy—not just dragging your sad butt behind you like a bug that got swatted-- but didn't die.

To Your Empowerment!—Phoenix Alexander

THE WAY OF THE PHOENIX